I AM

A MOTHER

D0756009

I AM
A MOTHER

Ella May Miller

SPIRE BOOKS

Fleming H. Revell Company
Old Tappan, New Jersey

Library of Congress Cataloging in Publication Data

Miller, Ella May.
    I am a mother.

    Bibliography: p.
    1. Mother and child. 2. Children—Care and hygiene. 3. Children—Management. 4. Family—Religious life. I. Title.
HQ772.M444   301.42'7   76-40345
ISBN 0-8007-8280-1

Contents

Preface

Being a mother is both beautiful and dangerous.

It is beautiful because of the new dimension a child brings to a mother's life. Those new joys of a child's total love, those many new insights into life and human relationships, as well as new responsibilities, enlarge and enrich a mother's life. It is dangerous because during those very early years, the baby absorbs all that's going on about him or her. The foundation for the child's future is being determined through absorbing the feelings, attitudes, interactions of the adults in the home. All this is beautiful when the child is surrounded with goodness, faith, and love, but it is dangerous when these qualities are absent. And there's no one monitoring mom's actions during the day.

I am fully aware that both parents—father and mother—are vital to a child's upbringing. The father needs to identify with the child in those early years, too, but because of a mother's biological makeup she is much closer to the baby in those early months and years—the prenatal period, infancy, and the toddler and preschool years. She spends more time with the child than does the father. Therefore, these closer relationships and more time with the baby naturally bequeath to her more responsibility and privileges.

The mother must know the child's basic needs and how to meet them adequately. She must be aware of the stages of growth and development and how to relate to the child in the best possible way.

Because mothering is so very important and crucial to our homes, our communities, our churches, and nation, I've written this book *I Am a Mother*. I share largely from my own experiences. Much of this material has come from my radio messages on the nationwide program called "Heart to Heart." I also share from others who have walked down the path of motherhood. I wish to give special recognition to Anna Kathryn Eby's assistance with the manuscript; to Peggy Landis who contributed much to Chapter 8, "Children and Good Reading"; to Alta Mae Erb, whose material appears in Chapter 6, "Creative Play"; to Mary Nell Rhodes for her careful editing; to Evelyn Sauder, my faithful secretary, and to a host of other persons who contributed directly or indirectly to this book. Many thanks!

I wish also to recognize another valuable source for many of the guidelines and principles I subscribe to. They come from the best book on child raising that we mothers could ever read—the Bible.

I Am a Mother is not a professional book based on the latest child-rearing methods. You can get that kind in any bookstore. This book is written basically from a personal viewpoint. I'm sharing basic principles, basic truths, and attitudes that can help any mother who is looking for aids in her important task and privilege.

The days of babyhood are quickly over. Childhood is soon gone. You can never replay the tape of childhood. What is done is done.

Now I know there are no perfect parents, no perfect mothers. I'm one of the imperfect ones. I do know that we make fewer mistakes when we can observe and learn from experience.

Experience, a willingness to apply ourselves, and faith in God—all help us to fulfill our task of raising sons and daughters to be positive citizens in both kingdoms—this world's and God's.

Happy mothering!
Ella May Miller

I AM

A MOTHER

1

Children Bring Joy

Two thousand years ago in ancient Rome, Cornelia, a great Roman lady, was asked by a friend to display her jewels. "Certainly," replied Cornelia. Calling her two sons in from play she proudly said, "These are my jewels."

Once while waiting four hours between flights at the Washington National Airport, I observed with pleasure a number of parents who were thoroughly enjoying their children. There was the young mother with two babies—I judged them to be about six weeks and twelve to fifteen months of age. Through all their cries and disturbances she was patient and loving, without one harsh word or sign of irritation.

Nearby was a couple, probably in their late thirties, with a lovely boy approximately four years old. How they enjoyed him! Carrying on a lively conversation with him, they answered all his questions and explained their plane schedule. In between questions he skipped around, and judging from his lip and arm movements, I decided he was playing a game. Then he'd traipse over to his mother who stroked his hair and kissed him lovingly.

A mother once told me that she's gotten a new approach to life since she and her husband became parents. She's received a whole new joy in the experience of caring for her child. She grew up thinking that fulfillment comes in doing one's own thing. However, since the baby came, she's been discovering fulfillment as a person—as a woman. She says it's also a joy to realize that her son has "brought a new discipline, a completely new area" into her life. "There has come the realization that just as I care for, love, and comfort my son, so God cares for, loves, and comforts me. My joy is becoming fuller and more complete."

It's not only small children who bring happiness to their parents. Teenagers can also bring joy, as the following incident indicates.

A group of women were getting together at Sarah's home. Some had already arrived and were in the kitchen sipping coffee. As I walked in, I noticed a tempting pie sitting on the counter with a folded piece of paper lying on top of it. I joined the friends in their lively chatter. Then one of them turned to Sarah and suggested that she show me what was written on the piece of paper.

Sarah took the paper off the pie and handed it to me, explaining that the night before she had prepared a crumb cake and put it in the oven to bake. It was late. Her fourteen-year-old daughter knew she was tired, so offered to take the cake out of the oven when it was done, and told Sarah to go to bed. Sarah did. When she came downstairs in the morning, she found the pie with the note on it. The note read:

Dear Mom:

You won't believe this (but you'd better get prepared). I took the cake from the oven when the timer went off. I let it cool ten minutes like the recipe said, then took it out of the pan. And, just my luck, it all fell to pieces. That's what that mess is on the plate.

I knew you wouldn't have time to bake anything in the morning so I decided to bake an apple pie. I don't know if it's good or not. You could serve ice cream with it. Or go out and buy something else.

While that was baking I straightened up the living room so you wouldn't have to do that in the morning.

Your loving daughter.

For lunch, we ate the pie without ice cream. It was delicious! I challenge any homemaker to make a flakier crust than did that fourteen-year-old girl, late at night, in a response of love for her mother!

Both Sarah and her husband were bubbling over with what their daughter had done. And rightly so! She brings them much joy in their daily relationships. For them, raising children is not an extracurricular activity or a sideline. Together, as a united team, they cooperate in the daily demands, responsibilities, privileges, and good times of being a family.

One godly grandfather, in describing the joy and comfort that his grown children bring to him, recounted the passage in Psalm 127 where the poet describes an old man going to the gate to confront his enemies. He has no fear because his children go before him. They bring him honor and security.

Children are a challenge to all parents. Parents can focus on the fun, the rewards, the joys, and satisfactions of each day, or they can focus on all the negative aspects. Authorities agree that their focus determines the kind of relationship between themselves and their children. The following responses illustrate the negative focus. One mother wails, "My two boys are so trying. I get depressed caring for them." Another says, "My children make me so nervous I finally end up in bed with a bad case of colitis." Another mother laments, "I resent my girl. She came twelve years after our last child." And finally this confession, "I have a beautiful eight-year-old daughter, but my six-year-old is pixie and ill-mannered."

In contrast, Julia and her husband focus on the positive. They are learning the joys children bring into their lives since they've changed their focus. Julia writes:

We're just beginning to enjoy what our boys, ages six and seven, enjoy. We never cared for parties, community and school activities. But recently, as a family, we entered into a school play (which ordinarily would have drained us). We encouraged our son's participation and helped him memorize his part. We made a special evening out of the occasion and thoroughly enjoyed it. The program was good; so was our son. We told him so. After it was all over we came home, still excited, but thrilled that together we enjoyed the event, especially our son's part. Our boys respond so lovingly and happily to our new appreciation for them.

From my own experience as a parent, I know children bring a new, thrilling dimension into a couple's lives. Our three little boys came to us within four years' time. At times I was discouraged with their racket and noise, their boisterous play, their mischief, their inexhaustible energy! Other days they brought much joy and love into our lives as parents.

However, as I look back on those never-to-be-relived days, there's much I would like to do over again.

I would be more patient with their many questions —which often irritated me.

I would laugh at a lot of their pranks and remarks —which I took too seriously.

I would spend more time with them in play and recreation—too often it was work.

I'd devote more time to constructive discipline— rather than on-the-spot judgments.

I would listen with greater interest to their childish

stories and reports of the day's happenings—too often these went in one ear and out the other.

I would take more time to show them—instead of just telling.

Some things I would not change—the nightly bedtime with a story, a prayer, and a goodnight kiss; the hours we spent together reading Bible stories and hunting verses in their own little Bibles; the money we invested in children's records and books—especially biographies of men who achieved for God and for their fellowmen.

I would not change those picture memories of bouquets of cactus flowers, of secret gifts and cards they made at school and behind closed doors, of those conversations around the table, of the games played while traveling by boat, by air or by car, of times recounting childhood stories and looking at family photos, or of the hours spent helping with homework.

Family relationship and affections are the principal sources of happiness and of a person's well-being. These mutual loves of husband and wife, of parents and children, of brothers and sisters also furnish the chief basis of our actions and the chief safeguards from evil.

The couple who accept children as a blessing receive a new sense of joy as they view their creative act of love fulfilled in each child. They become more united in a common purpose of caring for the child.

Sacrificing for children brings happiness, as both father and mother place the children's needs of love, security, and companionship above position, power, and possessions.

Children challenge parents with their honesty, their crystal-clear lives, their tender love, their quickness to forgive and forget wrongs, their remembrance of the good and kind, their implicit trust and simple faith.

Parents keep young as they search for answers, laugh and cry together with their children. Parents who teach children about God and His truths and guide children into noble character, into assuming responsibility, are the parents who keep in touch with true values of life.

As we teach, we learn. There comes the time when parents discover that in losing their lives for their children they have found life—richer, deeper, and more meaningful.

A professor working toward his doctorate in the area of school guidance comments, "I am convinced in the light of the wholesome adjustment I think I see in my children and in my students, that one of the biggest dividends for good in a person's life, one of the most abundant sources of satisfaction stems from the patience of helping a child develop to wholesome manhood or womanhood."

Jesus said, "Let children come to me, for of such is the kingdom of heaven . . . Unless you become as a little child, you cannot enter the kingdom of God." (*See* Luke 18:16, 17.)

Children bring joy!

2

Mother, I'm Coming!

A baby is a miracle!

The fertilized egg is about as big as the dot over the letter *i*. Yet it embodies all the genetic characteristics that will make the child a unique individual.

Immediately after fertilization changes take place in this egg. Around the nineteenth or twentieth day there are distinct grooves or ridges, and one end becomes the head. Within a few days, brain matter starts to fill that hollow end. Small buds that will become arms and legs soon appear on the embryo. By the thirty-first day, the rudimentary heart has started to beat. By the third month, this developing embryo is called a fetus. The fetus continues to develop until it is "mature" and ready for birth.

Whether the expectant mother has chosen to have the baby or whether it is unplanned, she *can* learn to love the unborn child that lies close to her heart.

The mother-to-be should realize that she's susceptible to irritations and annoyances because of minor pains, discomfort, physical awkwardness, and new and different kinds of fatigue and weariness. Some irrita-

tions are caused by emotional inadequacies or a new
dependence on others.

For the woman having her first baby there is the
profound realization that she will never be a little girl
again. As a mother she will move into the adult genera-
tion, and there is no turning back.

She might have fears concerning the aloneness of
labor and the loneliness of being at home with the baby,
particularly if she has previously been a career woman.
There will also be the new responsibility of restructur-
ing her time to an infant's schedule.

She may be alarmed about special cravings for certain kinds of food. Some of her questions might be:
"Will I be a good mother? Am I capable of being one?
How will my husband react to his father role? Will the
baby be normal? Can I breast-feed the baby? Will I
panic when I'm at home alone with the baby totally
dependent on me? How can I discern its needs?"

Such questions and fears are valid. The worst thing
is for an expectant mother to worry about her fears and
emotions and feel that she's abnormal. What she needs
is sympathetic help and reassurance.

If there are already children in the family, this calls
for special consideration and understanding also.

Mary, who already had a two-year-old daughter, was
concerned if her little girl would readily accept the
baby. Would there be jealousy or rejection?

Marge found her fourth pregnancy hard to accept.
She loved the three children she already had, but her

small home just didn't have room for another child. So until she was nearly four months pregnant, she pretended it wasn't true. Quietly, desperately she tried to forget what was happening. But one day she couldn't close her zipper, and she burst into tears, realizing there was no denying it—she was pregnant.

That night, after a tiring day, she went to bed. Lying there, relaxed, she felt that first fluttering of life within her. She shared the moment with her husband. They lay quietly thinking of the new tiny life within her waiting for a welcome, waiting to be born and loved.

Marge smiled to herself. "Tomorrow I'll find room in our house, now that I've made room in my heart."

Another mother worked full time during her first two pregnancies and participated in a hectic schedule of community and church activities. She lived under constant pressure, tensions, frustration, and exhaustion. Her babies were fussy and susceptible to many illnesses. When she became pregnant the third time, she had made some decisions:

I decided to take life easier. I dropped everything that created pressures and tensions. I became relaxed and secure. I had time to show caring, calm love. I began enjoying each day. I had time for Bible reading and prayer. My third baby was a good baby, slept well, and always woke up happy. Friends tell me that it just happened. She had a different personality. I know she does have her own unique personality—each child does—but both she and my fourth child, a boy, are more emotionally secure than the oldest sons. I'm not saying that every mother should do as I did, but this has been my experience.

Each mother must be honest with herself during this time. She must know and be ready to do what is necessary in order to have good emotional health. Consideration, kindness, and understanding from her husband and others helps the mother to accept her pregnancy, but she alone decides whether to wallow in self-pity or to accept the pregnancy with a positive attitude.

The expectant mother also needs to realize the importance of a nutritious diet, cleanliness, proper exercise, and rest. If she wants to breast-feed the baby, she'll begin to toughen her nipples in preparation for the baby to suck. She'll keep in regular contact with her doctor and follow his instructions.

If there already are children in the family, the parents will want to share the news with them. Their ages will determine how much and how soon. If possible, the children should be involved in specific preparation and planning as the time approaches for the mother's delivery.

Together, the father and mother will want to choose names for a boy or a girl. It is good to keep the name simple and to choose one that is quite commonly known. An unknown, unusual name may create problems for the growing child.

An expectant mother also prepares a layette, bassinet or crib, and adequate bedding. During the eighth month, she'll pack the suitcase for the hospital stay. It will include personal items for several days' stay, as well as the baby's take-home clothes.

The fears of childbirth frequently experienced by the mother-to-be can be quickly erased through adequate knowledge. She should feel free to share her fears with her husband, and together the couple should share them with her doctor.

In numerous communities there are classes for the expectant parents, fathers and mothers together. They are instructed about childbirth and acquainted with techniques and procedures that aid them during the birth. Many hospitals include the prepared husband in the excitement that is ahead by allowing him to become involved during labor. Here he can massage tense muscles and relieve his wife of physical stress. Most of all, he can protect her from the loneliness of labor.

Some hospitals will even allow the husband in the delivery room where he can celebrate the birth with his wife. Couples who share together in this way claim this is an experience of pure exultation that strengthens their own marriage relationship.

One father relates, "The intense joy of helping my wife to push and bring forth our twins, hearing their first cries and seeing the first struggles to adjust to their new world, is an experience more valuable than any other we have shared."

After the birth of her first child, a mother shared:

> With the six weeks of prepared childbirth classes behind, we could hardly wait to put what we'd learned to practice. My husband was as excited as I when that first contraction came. Through the whole experience, we worked as partners. We were brought closer together as husband and wife by the events of the birth, beginning with the timing of the first contractions and visiting our doctor to confirm the beginning of true labor. Then in the hospital—sitting together in the admitting room, the coaching and encouragement in labor, the first sight of that small head. Then the final announcement: "It's a girl!"
>
> The partnership is still continuing as we share the joys of each new day with our daughter. We feel that it was strengthened by the shared childbirth experience.

An older mother who had suffered from postpartum depression following the births of her first children proceeded through her third pregnancy with a great deal of apprehension. She was able to discuss her fears with her husband and her doctor. Together she and her husband studied the Lamaze method of childbirth. At the hospital her husband was allowed to remain by her side, and with his helpful encouragement she was able to have the baby without any anesthesia. This mother exulted:

To have a baby conceived in love and then to be born into a loving atmosphere with the baby's father beside me cradling my hand in his; to have a wonderful caring doctor and nurse; to hold the baby, this marvelous miracle of love and life; to be alert with all my senses participating—it was a gift which overwhelmed me. God must have been laughing on us, and I wanted to laugh right back. I wanted to shout praises from the Psalms. "Bless the Lord, O my soul! Sing! Clap! Leap! Oh, bless the Lord!" I felt like the lame man who picked up his bed and walked. I wanted to waltz all over the hospital! "Listen, everybody! We've had a baby!"

Many hospitals now allow the baby to room in with the mother and provide liberal visiting hours for the father. This acquaints both the mother and the father with their little one. The parents can begin to get used to the baby's personality and daily routine. With the help of nurses they can overcome that first awkwardness of handling and caring for their tiny baby. This gives them an excellent preparation for going home. Both mother and father can be calm as they help the older brothers and sisters to relate to the new baby.

Just as parents prepare for good physical care and protection, they also need to prepare for the spiritual nurture of the baby. This begins with the realization of what the child is. The baby is an individual, not a pet or a toy. There's a spirit within that physical person, a basic potential, and a unique personality that comes from God. Parents only cooperate with God in this creative act of forming a person.

It's a mysterious formation of substance and spirit, formed with a definite plan and purpose in life. This knowledge gives parents a beautiful anticipation of the coming birth. It gives them a sense of humility, of a dependence on God, and a sense of the need to cooperate with Him in rearing this child He has loaned to them.

The home atmosphere and the parents' relationship to each other very much determine the pattern the child's life will take.

Surely God was wise to give mom and dad nine months to prepare themselves, emotionally, physically, mentally, and spiritually.

3

Meeting Baby's Needs

The baby has arrived. The anticipation is over for the new mother. It is time to leave the security of the hospital and the assistance of the nurses. Now that helpless, tiny person is totally dependent on its mother and father.

"Parenthood arrives abruptly; it is the only major life role for which there is no preparation and it is irrevocable. . . . Parenthood (not marriage) forces young couples to take the last painful step into the adult world," says Dr. E. E. LeMasters.[1]

The couple who have learned to communicate openly and work through their problems together before the baby comes will find it much easier to help meet each other's needs at this time. The baby, this beautiful, sometimes terrifying little person, will most certainly bring about an upheaval in the daily routine. Parents must be prepared to be flexible as they work around these changes.

Even the best parents will have questions about the many unknowns, but they will be able to do selected reading concerning the different stages of normal development. At the same time, they must be sensitive to the fact that each child has its own rate of progress.

There is much said and written about the "blues" or postpartum depression. The new mother has enjoyed the delightful thrills and emotions of parenthood. She wants her baby and loves it with all her mother love, but eventually she'll feel the brightness begin to dim. She may imagine a cloud of depression hovering about her.

Much of the problem is due to fatigue. Some of the problem is due to emotional factors that emerge because of the intricate hormonal connections existing between the body and the mind. This can affect the mother's mental, emotional, and spiritual outlook.

The new mother questions her feelings about the baby who drastically changed her life, about her relationship with her husband, with her friends, and with groups she formerly was involved with. She must learn to recognize and admit these feelings. Expressing her feelings honestly and maintaining open communication with her husband does much to help her rise above her depression.

Around-the-clock responsibility for the new baby is demanding and fatiguing. Even though the father might be a novice at child care, his efforts to help, a good sense of humor, and sensitivity to his wife's moods will help to lighten the atmosphere. If there are older children in the family, they can learn to share the work load. Whenever possible, they should be involved in caring for the new baby. This will help to include them in their parents' love and time.

"It is particularly important for the new mother with other children to have some relief and relaxed adult company," says Dr. Edgar L. Engel.[2] Perhaps some arrangements could be made for part-time help during those first weeks. An evening out alone with her husband and an enjoyable hobby are also advisable.

The new mother can start to look forward to the pleasure of getting back her figure. Her doctor will recommend simple exercises to firm and tone her muscles, making good posture automatic.

Complete, firm healing of an episiotomy takes several weeks. Doctors generally suggest that sexual relations be curtailed until the incision is healed and the area has been examined at the mother's six-week checkup. The mother who bottle-feeds her baby may choose whatever method of birth control she prefers. However, the breast-feeding mother should not use birth control pills as this results in a decreased milk supply.

The new mother also needs to maintain spiritual health. She needs to keep close to the Creator of her new baby and allow her spirit to share with His Spirit.

The new father will encounter many adjustments. He, too, must make room in his heart and schedule for his child and work through his feelings. A father's attitudes greatly influence the mother's reactions.

One young mother felt resentment because her husband refused to change his life-style. After all, he thought, she was tied up with the baby, anyway. Besides, *she* had wanted the baby. It was her choice. He couldn't understand why she sometimes felt inadequate or depressed.

In contrast, Dee's husband sensed her apprehension and her physical weakness. Together they discussed these. When possible, he spent more time at home helping her with the baby. Dee was careful not to *demand* that he change the diaper, get the pacifier, or even do the housework. Instead, she shared her feelings about the baby with him. He wanted to become a part of her life with the baby during these new experiences.

Fathers who have taken prenatal classes with their expectant wives, who have been allowed to assist her in the labor room, and who share the excitement of the baby's delivery, quickly talk about "our baby." These experiences bring husbands closer to the wives and link them up with their children right away. Their interest and excitement in the new baby are greater.

Parents should learn that "babies are their own people," according to Dr. Stella Chess, a noted New York child psychiatrist. Women who have borne two or more children can find themselves baffled by the differences in their babies' behavior. Whereas one baby may have a quiet temperament, sleeping long hours and following a convenient schedule, allowing the mother to rest and pursue other interests, another baby might be "hyper," overreacting to noises or the moods of those around him. When the mother is tired or tense, she might find him to be impossibly jumpy or fussy. A baby might have eating and crying habits that leave him full of gas.

The parents can be helped as they listen to the advice of authorities and to older, more experienced couples. However, in the end, the new father and mother need to do what they feel comfortable with as they relate to the individual child. Parents are not a failure if the baby is fussy. They need to relate kindly to the difficult child. If they react anxiously or resentfully, they only increase his difficulties.

Some parents who have a high tolerance for noise do not get unduly upset by a crying baby. Other parents react anxiously and cannot get their own rest. Perhaps a grandmother or an older, reliable woman would be willing to care for the hyperactive baby for a day or a night. The mother could then get her rest, and the household could regain its equilibrium.

The physical care is necessary, but of greater importance is meeting the baby's emotional needs. He enjoys the warmth and closeness of the mother's body, her encircling arms, and the rhythmic heartbeats he had listened to for many months. He receives this naturally if he is breast-fed. If the mother gives a bottle instead, she should still hold him close, even after he can hold the bottle by himself. This close contact gives him a feeling of security.

"A baby can't get too much love," says psychologist Sidney Cohen of Los Angeles. The baby understands love through stroking, fondling, bathing, powdering, kissing, and hugging. In the first few months of life, these touching activities are the means of communicating love and security. Dr. Cohen believes that this need is as vital to the well-being and future emotional development of an infant as the feeding process.

The baby needs tender, loving care. Discipline comes later. He responds and reacts to the parents' emotions. If the parents are irritated, always in a hurry, or resentful, or neglect him when he cries, the child feels rejection. When they are relaxed, content, and happily meet his needs, he feels acceptance and love. Thus parents should use the daily routines of feeding, changing diapers, and bathing the baby as an opportunity to communicate love, instead of enduring these tasks as chores or duties.

The baby who is awake wants to be where you are. "But I can't get my work done!" mothers complain. There are ways to help you to combine baby care and work. Strap the baby in an infant seat on the counter beside you or in a carrying bag fastened to you. Accustom him to being in a playpen where he can watch you or other family members. This provides room for him to learn to roll over or crawl. During pleasant weather, the playpen can be placed out-of-doors in a safe spot. You will be surprised at how soon he can turn over. Never leave him alone on a bed, couch, or table.

In a couple of months the baby will enjoy brightly colored squeeze toys, especially the soft, lightweight animals with tails, legs, or necks on which he can get a good grip. His playthings will go straight to his mouth, so avoid toys with buttons, felt, or pieces of material that can find their way into his windpipe. Later on, the baby will enjoy playing with small pans, lids, measuring spoons, plastic containers, and other nonbreakable items in your cupboard.

But be careful—as your baby begins to explore, never allow him to play where you keep detergents, cleansers, and other toxic materials. It's best to keep such items out of reach.

Frequently relax with the baby, just to observe, to meditate, to sing, or share with him. Acquaint the infant with soft, soothing music. Begin with lullabies as you hold or rock him. Repeat verses and rhymes. Converse with him. Name objects as you care for him and play and relax together.

Allow him to be a baby. Don't try to push him into learning. Let him discover his toes, his hands, how to roll over, to crawl, to pull himself up, and to walk when *he* is ready.

Keeping a baby book can be fun. One mother jots down on her calendar significant happenings. Later, when time permits, she'll complete the baby book with interesting facts and photos. Another mother laid aside magazines, daily newspapers, and catalogues that came at the time her baby was born. These are mementos that will be of interest to her child in the years to come.

Motherhood is more than a profession. It is a way of

life. Developing understanding and loving relationships as you meet your child's needs is your greatest responsibility. On this firm foundation of security you continue to build, as will his teachers, friends, and ministers in later life.

The child is more than someone merely to train or educate. Primarily he is a person with a soul, a spirit, and emotions. His character for his future is being built as he observes and imitates your words and actions, your faith and trust in God.

4

Baby Becomes a Toddler

We experienced the delightful privilege of having our grandson, Obadiah, with us one summer when he was between eight and one-half to eleven months of age. Caring for a child again reminded me that I had forgotten how fast a baby develops. He was constantly experimenting with the wheels of his toy truck and baby stroller. He placed blocks in a plastic bucket and dumped them out. He swung doors and shoved things that shouldn't be moved. He tasted his toys, shoes, or books and tried to walk. Up he bounced after a tumble to start all over again. He was just beginning to climb the stairs and to discover the delights of splashing in the bathroom.

He talked his own language, frequently in long sentences and sometimes in paragraphs with his own voice inflections. He learned to say "nana" for banana and soon associated this with all food. Any animal, even the plastic honey bear sitting on the breakfast table, was a "woo-woo." Of course his vocabulary included "Da-da" and "Ma-ma." A toy car or truck was a "brr." He waved "bye-bye."

As a happy baby who smiled, cooed, and gurgled, Obadiah had been the center of his parents' and grandparents' attention. Now he was becoming a toddler, quickly moving from one spot to another, almost before his mother or daddy could detect it. His curiosity and need for exploring took on new dimensions. His home and surroundings needed to be made into a place where he could be comfortable and safe.

How can a mother supply the needs of a little investigator such as this and still get her work done? A toddler enjoys older children. One solution would be to have an older child help to watch him during your busy moments.

There will be times when there is no older child to help and when you can't watch your toddler. Place the playpen equipped with various objects and toys in your work area. As the child sees you and hears your occasional words of love and concern, or as you hand him lids and old pots and pans, he might be satisfied for a short time. This affords a close contact between you and him, and at the same time it allows you to do your tasks.

Most mothers have found that the best solution is to cut back on the amount of work they used to feel was necessary. A happy baby is more important than the neatest home.

As the toddler's field of action expands beyond himself, he becomes aware of the existence of other people and activities that demand your attention and time. He learns that his own needs and desires must fit into the family schedule, and he slowly becomes a part of the family's routine. This does not happen easily. He cries and bangs on his high chair because he wants his food *now*. He resents gates and barriers that limit him. His temperament varies rapidly. One minute he is running away, and the next moment he wants to be held.

The active toddler has no concept of what is his and what belongs to the other children he is playing with, so he grabs any toy he wants. He is self-willed and determined and sets no limits for himself.

Or the toddler may have a quiet, less aggressive personality and allow other children to push him around while he cries for his mother's protection. In either case, it is not fair to label the child as "bad" if he's boisterous and full of initiative, or "good" if he is more passive and easily contented. He is only acting according to his natural behavior.

The timid toddler will eventually learn how to be more assertive. His mother will do him a favor by being casual and sympathetic concerning his dilemmas rather than becoming too emotionally charged. She needs to support him rather than to take over.

The more aggressive child calls for much understanding and patience. Unfortunately, this is frequently the period when he gets the least. It is better for his mother to be the friendly boss than to fight it out on his own age level. Commanding and demanding, shouting him down, slapping or shaking him will make him feel rejected. Your aim is not to break his will but to help him to learn to use it wisely. It is best to teach him obedience in a positive way. Show him how to play and to share with others. Show him what he can touch or have and what is off limits.

Because the child is now able to walk, too many parents expect him to act as an adult, but he will act as a child because he is a child, and he needs to be approached as one.

Parents have a tendency to force the toddler to become independent too quickly. Certainly he will learn to feed himself and dress himself, but he should not be rushed. Invent games to play with him while teaching him to pick up his blocks and toys. Continue to cuddle and rock him and have carefree, relaxed play-times. A wise mother dares not shove aside love and affection.

The older toddler from sixteen months and up can learn there are limits and controls. He can be taught to stay out of drawers and cupboards, away from the sewing machine and other places unsuited to his needs. He learns best from a positive approach.

One mother walked with her two-year-old around the edge of the yard, telling him that beyond this he could not go. She didn't threaten him but kept an eye on him. He stayed within the yard for a week, and then one day he wandered outside. She again took his hands and walked within the limits of his playground. However, the second time he walked away she spanked him. That was the end of his running off.

Most children do not learn this easily. One mother of an excessively active toddler found that long walks had a soothing effect on both her son and herself. When her self-control would begin to crack, she would bundle her son into her backpack. An hour later they would come back from their tramp refreshed and in good spirits with each other.

Another mother found that singing and dancing with her child to the tunes on his records cleared the atmosphere.

Toilet training comes at this stage of a child's life. Most children are not physically able to control their body functions before they near their second birthday. Attempts to train too early will merely create unnecessary frustrations.

Parents set the stage during these early years for communication and relationships with their child for the time he becomes a teenager. Ashley Montagu, a noted anthropologist, says that it's a mistake to think we can pump the right information into Junior's head so that he'll grow up to be a decent fellow. The most necessary element of education and right training is "unconditional love which is not offered as a bribe to eat cereal or to keep on good behavior."

Of course love disciplines, but the child needs to know that his parents' love will be there even when he isn't happy and obedient and feeling good. If love is withheld when he is bad or when his spirits hurt, he will learn falsely that *doing* is more important that *being*.

After a few rounds of bedtime discipline, one small fellow snuggled up close and pressed his head against his daddy's chest, hard. He wanted to be absolutely certain that his daddy still loved him.[3]

Consistency in disciplining is important. The child who can do anything he wants to do one day and then gets punished for doing the same thing the next day is surely bewildered. Parents should be with their child enough during the day to teach him their values. Otherwise, he might be learning from someone who differs drastically from them in these areas.

Parents need to be united, supporting each other even when they may differ. In a contented, cheerful home atmosphere the toddler learns easily. When the members of the family are considerate of each other, the child will absorb kindliness. If the parents genuinely like other people, the child will like people too, and he will not have difficulty with the surface manners.

Our words and deeds need to be wrapped in love. The source of love is God. When you find love and patience running out, relax a moment and share your need with God. His supply of love is always available.

5

Enjoy Your Preschooler

It was Christmas season, and once more the Browns were harmonizing all the old familiar Christmas carols, including the line, "Shepherds shake off your drowsy sleep." The next morning, mother overheard her three-year-old lustily singing, "Shepherds shake off your trousers and sleep!"

A four-year-old opened the door to a salesman and explained, "My mother doesn't eat too much butter. The reason she is so fat is because she is going to have a baby!"

The parents are entertaining a very proper guest when their four-year-old amiably breaks into conversation with, "The water in our toilet came out all over the floor."

"This is the age when I could just keep Maria for a pet," a charmed father exclaimed about his three-year-old. "She's potty-trained, slightly civilized, and just as cute and frisky as a puppy."

Yes, mothers, this is the time for relaxed schedules and lots of fun times and laughter. In a couple of years the preschooler will be in school and away from home for most of the day.

Most parents will also admit that life is sometimes a battle at this age. The preschooler pushes them to the limits of their wits with his endless adventures and their having to watchdog all his activities.

The child has more questions than you have time or patience for in your busy schedule, and you catch yourself thinking, "I can't wait till I can send him to school all day and have some peace and quiet around here!"

No mother can laugh and be jolly all the time. When you hit a low, you can talk to God about your feelings. Sometimes the counsel of an older, more experienced mother will be encouraging and helpful.

Often it's hard to know whether preschoolers are merely going through a stage or if it's an urgent problem to be handled immediately. Bed-wetting, tantrums, and jealousy are common stages that children go through at this age.

Like all of us, a child needs to sense his own self-worth. If Johnny is made to feel that he's in the way or that you don't have time for him, it can be damaging. Preschoolers especially need to know that they are loved and accepted by both father and mother and that they help to contribute to their parents' happiness.

Preschoolers are often content if they can work alongside you in your chores, or play near you. When Johnny becomes irritable and demanding, stop and give him ten minutes of your undivided attention. Read some books together, or build a castle, or enjoy a little tea party with him. After that, he'll be more content to play by himself.

It is best to give him the attention he needs *before* he starts throwing his toys. If he gets attention and love only by being naughty, he'll soon learn to throw tantrums to make you listen.

Remember to be consistent in disciplining the child. Follow the rules you have set up. Giving in to Johnny's demand to stand on his chair while eating will confuse him when you say "no" next time. Also, if he receives one message from his mother and another from his father, he will be frustrated. Good communication and cooperation between you and your husband are important. It is important, too, that the baby-sitter know your rules and routines and be dependable enough to stick to them.

The world as your preschooler sees it can open windows for you to a delightful, magical place. Four-year-old Todd told his mother, "Look, Mommy, the sun is playing hide-and-seek with the clouds." Listen to your child's jabber, the rhymes, songs, and games he invents. It can often brighten your day!

A friend of mine especially enjoys preschoolers. Viola says, "We live near a woods, so the children and I take walks. It's one thing to walk in the woods by yourself and quite another to walk with a child. We tread softly, listening for sounds."

Children need that intimate contact with growing

life. If you can have your own vegetable garden or live in the country where the child has access to meadows or woods, he is fortunate indeed. Pets to care for and farm animals to watch teach him to respect another aspect of life.

The mother of an apartment child will have to look for ways to expose her child to nature. A daily trip to a city park is not a waste of time. Houseplants, goldfish, and parakeets cannot bark or purr with affection, but they can teach a child to be gentle and sensitive as he helps to care for them.

Three-, four-, and five-year-olds need to have a lot of physical activity. Provide a place in the basement or in some part of the house where the child is free to exercise. Allow him to play outside as much as possible. Suzy seems to be always running, jumping, and hopping around. This kind of play allows her to develop muscles and limbs.

Play is the preschooler's work and occupies most of his waking hours. A variety of play items and things to do need to be available, but this does not mean that the mother needs to suggest or direct the child's activities all the time. He needs an opportunity to find things to do on his own in order to develop fully his five senses.

Toys needn't be expensive or elaborate. Building blocks, crayons, a sandbox, a ball, a second-hand trike, simple dolls, and modeling clay are playthings that allow for creative, unstructured play. A four-year-old is too young for the strain of tiny, tedious playthings.

Basically, let the child play with the toys he likes to play with. If your Bobby wants to play with dolls, don't worry. Many little boys enjoy playing with dolls as much as their sisters do.

Our little girl soon preferred her brothers' toys to her own. For her first birthday we presented her with a toy car. I so much wanted it to be a baby doll! There were no child specialists, nor did I have child-care books with me to consult in our isolated area in South America. Her daddy thought it was all right, so we based our decision on common sense. If she prefers a car, a car she'll have. To my pleasure, the dolls came later and were well accepted, loved, and "mothered."

Four- and five-year-olds are able to come up with surprising works of art. Encourage your child to draw pictures of his own. This is a more creative experience than to force him to follow the lines of a coloring book. It doesn't matter if you can't figure out what he's drawn. A child's creative urges can easily be discouraged if he feels his pictures must always make sense to an adult.

The child of three to five is just beginning to think for himself. The ideas that pop into four-year-old Sherry's head give her much self-satisfaction.[4] Her curiosity is a most wonderful tool. With it she finds out all kinds of things about herself and her world.

The preschooler's alert mind needs much stimulation. Reading aloud to your child not only stimulates his mind but also contributes to his feelings of emotional attachment to you. If you can't afford many books or records, you can borrow from your public or church libraries. A trip to the public library is a special treat for preschoolers.

If you get pleasure out of good reading and taking care of your books, your child will absorb these attitudes. Don't push him to begin reading too soon. He will know when he is ready.

If your child is busy in creative play or easily absorbed in books, you will not need to resort to the TV as a cheap baby-sitter. TV watching is too passive for active, growing preschoolers. They need to be stimulated by a real world.

Preschoolers need a balance of time alone, with you, and with other children. They need to discover things for themselves, in a relaxed atmosphere. Let them enjoy their play, and you'll find yourself enjoying it too!

What about nursery school for the three- and four-year old? Is this type of activity a necessary experience? Not even authorities can agree on this controversial subject, so it's important for parents to decide what is best for their own children.

Even the best nursery school cannot take the place of home but can only add to it. Some children have easy access to playmates and can learn at home how to cooperate and enjoy the company of other children. Many homes also have space to provide children with interesting, unstructured play activities. In addition, the child's world is expanded as his parents read to him, or as they take walks together in park or woods. They can also expose him to places of interest in his city or town, such as the fire station, the post office or a bank. Thus he will already be receiving many of the benefits of a nursery school.

Mothers do need time away from preschoolers. You'll be a better mother if you take the effort and expense of getting out once in a while. Several mothers I know take turns caring for each other's three- and four-year-olds. Each mother has one free afternoon a week.

The day will come when your preschooler is finally old enough to go to school. Nancy described her mixed feelings about sending her five-year-old Larry off to kindergarten for the first time:

> It makes me feel kind of funny. For the first time Larry is out of my control. I don't know what he is learning or hearing or doing. All I can do is trust we have instilled in him the right values and let him go. Letting go is really a hard part of motherhood. When Larry comes home from school, he is in another world for a little while, a world I'm not a part of.

Yes, the hardest part of preparing a child for school is letting go but still being there when the child needs you. When your child does adjust to going to school, you will be pleased that he is mature enough to get along without you.

In trying to keep up with a child's physical, social, and mental needs, it is easy to neglect his spiritual needs. The preschool age is the best time for a child to start learning about God's love. Little children can begin to understand that there's a special Person who *always* cares for them, protects them, and loves them.

Meeting spiritual needs is more than just saying a prayer at mealtime or reading a Bible story at bedtime. Your child can be reminded constantly of God's love and presence through nature, through discipline, or when he faces fears of nighttime, of storms, or of being left alone.

As your child hears you giving thanks to God for the day's simple blessings, as he sees you asking for guidance in the ordinary petty problems, and as you seek forgiveness for your besetting sins, he will be learning that God is interested in the smallest details of his life.

6

Creative Play

How much time do you allow your children for play? Do you think play is important for them?

I had almost forgotten how essential play is for children until I observed twenty-month-old Bobby yesterday. He loaded the wagon with some odds and ends and smaller toys he had discovered. He pulled it with the tractor, then unloaded it. He continued this procedure for a long time.

Later he became interested in a marble game and was fascinated watching the brightly colored marbles roll. He enjoyed listening to the noise.

Play, play, play—that's Bobby's interest as it is every child's.

Authorities lament the fact that many modern parents don't allow the child to be a child. They try to make him grow up as quickly as possible. Play isn't tolerated. Dr. Bruno Bettelheim, the noted child psychologist, says: "If we gave children the opportunity to play, maybe some of them would not be driven to compensate for time lost in childhood by playing 'revolution' or 'cops and robbers' in their twenties."[5]

Other parents are pressured to program every minute of their child's play. This can destroy his own creative imagination. Or it may become purely entertainment.

We recognize that play is very important, beginning early in life. But why? What does it have to do with growing up?

The baby learns about himself and about his world through play. It's important that he play much in order to develop into healthy, happy adulthood.

In his play a child experiments with his environment. He tries out his powers, but he accomplishes something pretty basic—he is learning. He distinguishes himself and others. The baby begins playing with his fingers and toes. He touches his mother's face, hands, and body. He discovers his environment. He begins through random movements of his arms and legs. He eventually is able to grab a toy or object and retain it in his hands while his arms and legs continue moving.

This is a complicated process, suggests Adele Franklin, director of All-Day Neighborhood Schools in New York. The tiny baby soon begins to experiment with sitting up, with standing, with picking up things with his fingers. He moves things about as he touches and tastes. He discovers that some things make a noise if he bangs them together or hits them on the side of his crib or on the tray of his high chair or throws them on the floor. He never stops trying out everything around him, including himself.

He learns about cause and effect. Liquids such as water, milk, or orange juice can be poured. Sand can be poured also. Blocks can be piled up, and when they are knocked down, they make a wonderful noise.

A child comes to us utterly helpless. God seems to have planned it that way, so we mothers and fathers can have the beautiful privilege of guiding the child's learning.

Parents hear much about reading readiness. It means simply that a child is ready to begin to learn the intricate skills involved in reading after he has learned to use language and understand the meaning of words. Through play experiences, he gains the concepts behind the words he hears. Through play and handling many different kinds of materials, he gains the ability to recognize shape, form, and color.

The young child enjoys cuddly toys and dolls. I mean a soft cuddly doll, not one that wets, or has real hair, or has a boyfriend. Toys should be carefully chosen. Look for toys with nontoxic paint and no sharp corners or edges. Wooden playthings are preferable to metal toys. Complicated toys are for grown-ups.

Blocks are for play and for learning. With these a child can create endlessly—a castle, a house, a barn, an airport, and so on.

Many toys on the market are so structured that they dictate the one activity they can be used for. What a difference between a wind-up toy that does only one thing and a wagon suitable to the child's size that he can use in many ways. Parents should furnish materials for imaginative play that allow great freedom in their uses.

Dr. Benjamin Spock says that children aren't satisfied to obey the directions of the inventor or manufacturer of a toy. They like "to express their own feelings, create their own dramatic situations, and make their own inventions . . . the less specific it is, the more it stimulates a child's imagination."[6] He suggests that blocks are the most stimulating and absorbing playthings of all. Children enjoy them from ages one to twelve.

Barbara says their son showed little interest in the toys they bought him. She came up with an answer to the "useless expense of many toys for toddlers." She covered a medium-sized box with brightly patterned adhesive paper and placed in it homemade treasures—bits of colored cellophane, bows from packages, plastic bottles, a round salt box with the bright label still on, plus worn-out colored shirts and brightly colored empty boxes. For hours on end her son enjoyed filling the box and emptying it. I remember how our children loved to play with boxes. They created trains, houses, cars, and whatnot out of them.

When I was a little girl, we would empty the big bucket of clothespins on the floor and then let our imaginations run loose. With no less than five playing together, we had a variety of ideas.

A child's play is highly imaginative. And much of his

play is imitating what he sees and hears other family members doing. He may try to be the mother doing regular daily housework, or the father going to business or driving the car. The grocery man or even the garbage collector may catch his fancy. To act out many roles, he uses his toys or an empty box as important props in his game of make-believe.

Boxes of cardboard and wood of all sizes, shapes and forms can be used. The child architect can stack boxes on top of one another, line them in a row, set them on end, and with his imagination change them into a boat, house, garage, cage, stage, zoo or whatever his fancy calls for. He can climb into a wooden crate or tumble it around the yard, giving himself a feeling of mastery within his world . . . .

Save your empty food containers so that your children can play food store. A cylindrical oatmeal box is perfect for a doll's cradle. All the little mother needs to do is to tape on the lid and cut out a portion of the box. . . .

Children who want to be carpenters can easily build furniture with a hammer, a few nails, a saw and some wooden boxes. They can have fun covering boxes with cloth or paper to make bedroom chairs and dressers.[7]

When my sons were small, I used to take empty, cylindrical oatmeal boxes, paste on the lid and cut a tiny hole at either end through which I drew a heavy cord. I hung these around their necks, and with smooth sticks for drumsticks they would march around our house in time to their tempo until their improvised drums gave out.

At play, the child is inventive and alert in solving problems. His play is also self-expression. He acts out his ideas and his feelings, and he learns about other people's ideas and feelings.

"But what about going along with the child's fantasy?" you question. "His toy animals often become real people."

As parents, we need to respect imaginative play— sometimes even enter into the child's fantasy. A five- or six-year-old can recognize the fact that he's been pretending.

Sometimes children are confused between reality and the make-believe world they've created. But here's where we can help them to make this distinction. We should remind them that they have been pretending. After the incident—say, when the child is washing before a meal or getting ready for bed—talk about the fun it was to pretend, but now he's Billy, or she's Sally, and suggest that sometime later there'll be a chance to pretend again.

As important as play is, children should be able simply to do nothing at times. Children need unscheduled time to watch the clouds, the stars, the trees, and the birds. They need the freedom to absorb a gentle summer rain, to pretend, to daydream, and to relax with a pet if they wish to do so. Or just to be alone.

In her children's book, *Evan's Corner,* Elizabeth Starr Hill writes about sensitive six-year-old Evan who lived along a noisy, busy street, up four flights of steep stairs in two rooms with his father, mother, three sisters, and two brothers. Evan wanted a place of his own where he could be alone, where he could enjoy peace and quiet, and where he could waste time if he liked. His mother suggested that he choose one corner for himself. Evan looked at the corner with the interesting crack in the wall and at the one with the pretty edge or rug. The one he finally chose for his own had a nice small window and a bit of polished floor. Evan shared his corner with a lacy weed that he planted in his toothbrush glass, a small crate for his piece of furniture, and a pet turtle. "That baby turtle had the scrawniest neck. Its feet were big and ugly. Its eyes were merry and black. If a turtle could smile, that turtle was smiling."[8] Evan found contentment in these less than ideal circumstances because his family respected his need.

The child needs play to develop muscles and coordination. Such play begins with his movements in the crib. Before many months, he begins climbing and pulling objects and toys. As he grows, you'll want to provide for outside play—a swing, sandbox, slide, climbing bars. If you have no space outside, set up some play equipment in the basement or playroom.

A two- or three-year-old enjoys playing beside

another child if each has his own toys. At this age they can't play together in the sense of sharing toys.

A child needs to play with children of his own age. Children learn from each other. They get much pleasure from companionship. They also need some playtime with older children. From them they learn about taking the lead, or following, about sharing, giving and receiving.

Dad and mom will need to plan play activities with the child and for the entire family to enjoy doing together. Activities of this kind provide fun and learning experiences and help to build the feeling of family unity and belonging. This is so important for the growing child.

Overdirecting can stifle children's creativity. A teacher was introducing a group of children to modeling clay. She showed them how to make a snake, and each child in turn made a snake. The children never made anything else. The teacher said the children were not interested in clay.

"Rigid authority depreciates ideas offered by children."[9] There is no need for adults to evaluate, grade, or mark every creation. Children learn by trial and error. Creative children work hard. They don't always succeed at once.

Richenda Ellis says that to be creative, children must feel that they are accepted and valued. They must be free to be themselves and to express their own ideas, knowing that these ideas will also be valued. Mrs. Ellis calls this approach "Creativity through confidence."

The preschooler should be given large sheets of clean paper to color on when his mother is not watching. Freed from all outside pressures or fears, he will do things never thought possible and in his own way. When he has finished drawing, his mother's wise comment should be, "Tell me about your picture." Her attitude will show her joy and acceptance of her child.

Each child needs space for his activities, even in a small house. Houses are for children's living. Can the railroad track which extends through several rooms be left up for several days' use?

There should be materials available with which to use the senses, media for expression in the arts, tools with which to cut, to dig, to build, to play in water and sand. For example, play in water calls for pitchers, funnels, soap flakes, straws, sponges and objects to float.[10]

A mother recently wrote in a popular magazine about her attempt to teach her children and the neighborhood children the game "Kick the Can." Despite her careful instructions and her help, they couldn't follow, nor were they interested.

When she asked her children if they liked the game, her son replied, "It's OK, but there aren't any good places to hide." She echoed, "He was right."

In the suburbs there are lovely homes and lawns,

"but there are no wild places left—no field ragged with weeds, no vacant lots, no woods, no narrow alleys, not even a dead-end street . . . or graveyard."

To this mother, however, the curcial question is: "If our children no longer have . . . secret places to hide, do they also lack the comfort of having a firm and welcoming base? Part of the game was our daring to leave the security of the telephone pole and venture out into the shadowy night, our fierce joy in racing back to it, safe, home, free."[11]

In spite of her beautiful lawn or lack of lawn, the wise mother will try to see that her child has a frequent chance to play in a park or a meadow or woods. Somewhere there must be space for children to leapfrog and chase each other's shadows.

Says Joan Beck:

"Nurturing your child's creativity is one of the most delightful privileges of parenthood." The creative child living in a rich Christian atmosphere can have strong confidence in God. He has found that God made a good earth and has provided an abundance of pleasant experiences. He does not have to conform to others' patterns to be happy. He is enthusiastic about living. Seeing this growth can be every parent's delight.[12]

KIND OF HOUSE

The kind of house that I grew up in
Was one you could chase a scraggy pup in,
And let old Tabby sleep on your bed.
This house had the smell of baking bread,
And linen fresh from the wind-blown line,
And a potbellied stove burning pitchy pine.
The rugs were worn on the creaky floors
Of the many rooms. But the rooms had doors,
And the doors would shut so a child could lie
With the cat by a windowful of sky
And read or dream or stare at a bird.
For here was a house where nobody's heard
Of being adjusted: you yelled and fought
And worked and loved. And you sang a lot.
And growing up in this house was such
That you rarely noticed the process much.[13]

GEORGIE STARBUCK GALBRAITH

7

Children Want Discipline

The four boys across the aisle from me on the train were the center of attraction in that car. They were like stairsteps in age from about four to ten and wore identical Davy Crockett shirts, trousers, and moccasins. For some time the little fellows entertained each other with seemingly nothing. For a diversion they would occasionally trip down the aisle one at a time to get a drink. Gradually their play developed into a friendly tussle, and they began getting noisier as they scuffled, bumping into their mother. The father instantly issued his orders, and the boys obeyed without a protest.

After a short period of quiet play, the boys again became rowdy. This time the father roughly swatted the offenders in the appropriate places. We passengers gasped, but without a whimper the fellows settled down once more to quiet play. Soon the father pulled down a box from the luggage rack and from it handed a Davy Crockett coonskin cap, complete with the tail, to each boy. For the rest of the morning they quietly entertained each other, with the father entering into their play.

We passengers could enjoy those boys because they had learned the meaning of discipline at an early age. The parents enjoyed each other and their sons. They were consistent in their discipline and administered it with love and concern.

Children lack wisdom and experience and are not capable of making the wisest decisions. The Bible says, "Foolishness is bound in the heart of a child, but the rod of correction shall drive it far from him" (Proverbs 22:15).

In contrast to this, another mother shared her experience with a family of three boys who came to visit her.

They were barely inside the door when two of them were banging frightfully on the piano and dinner gong, and the third was going through my cupboards looking for something to eat. They habitually stormed about so that adults could hardly carry on a conversation. . . .

We do our children no favor by permitting them to degenerate into insolent, self-centered, unmanageable persons heedless of instruction. Joey needn't be allowed to fuss and pout when he can't have his way. I refuse to comply with my own son's otherwise reasonable request if he presents it in the form of a rude demand.[14]

Before parents can gain respect from their children they must have respect for themselves. The parents' sense of guilt or insecurity tends to get in the way of easy management of their child. The working mother may feel that she is neglecting her child. The mother home from the hospital with a new baby wants the older child to feel secure. Parents who have just moved, making it necessary for their children to attend a new school, worry about their offsprings' adjustment.

The parents who feel guilty are often trying to be patient and sweet-tempered when their overworked patience is really exhausted and the child is, in fact, getting out of hand and needing some definite correction. Or they are vacillating when the child needs firmness. The child behaves worse and worse as if he were saying, "How bad do I have to be before somebody stops me?" Eventually the parents' patience snaps. In the heat of anger they punish the child. Ashamed of losing their temper, they allow their child to punish them by being rude. Once more the cycle begins.[15]

Four-year-old Nan whined and fussed all morning. She refused to color in her new book, to play with the dolls, or to have a tea party. In spite of Mother's threats, she repeatedly opened the oven door to peep at the cake. Finally in exasperation Mother jerked her from the floor, slapped her smartly, and laid Nan on the bed. To her astonishment, Nan sobbed, "I wish Daddy were home. He'd make me listen."

The spoiled child is not happy even in his own home. Out in the world he will find that he is disliked for his selfishness. He will either continue being unpopular or learn the hard way how to be agreeable.

Parents can stand up for themselves while still feeling friendly, if they have a healthy self-respect. Phyllis McGinley, the Pulitzer Prize winner, recalled the "patient, wistful voice" of a woman sitting next to her in the park. "Mother wishes you wouldn't," she was repeating monotonously to her frail four-year-old. "Mother doesn't like to be hit in the head with a dump truck." Phyllis went on to say:

> The casual mother would have seen the dump truck coming and calmly confiscated it. Even I, in my benighted day, owned one abiding faith—that I was brighter and a good deal stronger than any four-year-old. If anybody got bruises from lethal toys around our house, it wasn't going to be me."[16]

Phyllis McGinley also says that the secure, casual mother seldom nags and argues.

> She does not have to be told, as I was by an eight-year-old daughter, that argument defeats itself at times. "Oh, Mommie," she burst out once when I was reasoning with her over some childish lapse, "why don't you just tell me not to, and stop *explaining* at me?"[17]

Parents are sometimes victims of the philosophy that to say "no" will destroy their relationship with the child. So they resort to evasive answers such as "We'll see," or "Maybe," or they give the choice piece of dirty work to their partner by saying, "Ask Daddy." A wise mother who became aware that such a practice existed in her home consulted the Bible and found that God issued many negative statements as well as positive ones. She changed her tactics and began firmly and kindly to say "no" when it was necessary, without any apologies. As a result, relationships within her family became more pleasant.

Parents need to exercise discipline when their children make unnecessary demands, or if they can't afford it when children want to have the same things or to do the same things as other children they know. Children are very clever at pressuring each other and their parents. "My mother will let me if your mother will let you." The child must learn that different families have different values. The mother shouldn't automatically say "no" without even thinking of what her child is saying. She also needs to consider if a principle will be compromised by saying "yes."

Sometimes an acceptable alternative can be provided. Six-year-old Katrina begged for a teenage doll for Christmas. Her girl friends were taking their dolls to school to play with during the recess break. Katrina's friends said her mother was mean for not giving her the doll. Katrina's parents wanted their child to enjoy "little girl" pleasures. They did not approve of the Hollywood image of the big-bosomed, glamorous dolls.

Of course, a six-year-old would have had trouble understanding all those abstractions, so instead of a lot of explaining, Katrina's mother got to work. She made her little girl a large, beautiful set of Raggedy Ann and Andy dolls for Christmas, with "I love Katrina" embroidered on their hearts. Katrina was delighted. When she went back to school, she took her dolls with her. The other children said, "Wow! Katrina, you have a smart mother!" Everyone wanted to play with her dolls.

Discipline means teaching. Parents teach their child by example when they show genuine consideration for each other. The child absorbs kindliness. If the parents are animal lovers, the child will not torment his puppy because he will be absorbing their values. When parents interact with a variety of friends and are respectful of the rights and property and individuality of other people, the child learns these attitudes.

How rewarding to hear a child's unsolicited "thank you" and "I'm sorry," or his pleasant conversation with a guest, or his sympathetic remarks as he helps a younger brother, not because he has been taught these expressions like memorized formulae, but for the most part through unconscious example.[18]

Rules and limits are necessary. Here are some guiding principles that may be helpful towards more effectively disciplining children when they disobey:

1. Say what you mean and then abide by it. If you

tell Junior to be home ten minutes after school is dismissed, see that he obeys. This implies a moment of deliberation for you before making a new rule.

2. There must be consistency. Don't allow one thing today when you're feeling fine and forbid it tomorrow because you're feeling tired and crabby.

3. Either forgive or punish an offense; never resort to threats. Too frequently threats are forgotten by the parents or continually repeated but never fulfilled.

4. Both father and mother must agree to uphold each other's decisions and commands. If different opinions exist, these should be discussed privately.

5. Follow God's rule to *forget* after the offense is dealt with. Don't retain an ill feeling or grudge against the little fellow.

6. Discipline is for the child's good. To punish a child unkindly for accidentally spilling the milk is merely giving vent to your feelings.

7. Have long-range goals to help you in molding the child's character. This will give you a broader perspective as you encourage favorable traits and curb the undesirable ones.

8. Firm discipline must be accompanied by warm love, lots of fun, and kindness.

9. Effective discipline requires much time, thought, patience, and prayer.

10. We must be examples of a disciplined life by our submission to God's order and rules for our own happy, contented, and successful living.

Obedience to father and mother is the first step in enabling the child to learn self-control and the ability to live constructively outside of his home. Ultimately this can lead him to submission and obedience to God.

An awareness of God's love for us makes us want to accept His authority, makes us want to please Him. It's a fortunate child who early learns that lesson in his own home.

8

Children and Good Reading

In the eighteenth century *New England Primer* there
is a crude woodcut of a little child reading. Opposite the
picture is the couplet:

> My book and heart
> Shall never part.

We are very much a part of all the books that we
have met, and on the pages of our hearts it is easy to
read a gladsome rhyme left over from Mother Goose
days, a line of poetry that said so well what we have
always known but never could express, a powerful bi-
ography of a life that has challenged ours, a witty re-
mark, a promise from the Bible.

It is difficult to imagine what our daily lives would
be like without books. Because we know what books
can do for us, we covet these same advantages for our
children.

It is not too early for expectant parents to start planning ahead for their children's library. It is good to be
fortified with long-range plans for your child's reading

material. One newly married couple gave each other gifts of their favorite children's books on special occasions such as Easter or Valentine's Day.

Today's children live in a complex world of rockets, television, and radar. Their world has Africa and China for close neighbors and looks to the stars as goals for possible future journeys. Most of these children know about tensions and war. Some are growing up in single-parent families, and some have little contact with grandparents, aunts, uncles, and the rest of the extended family.

Good books can give our children the information they want and need. They can broaden our children's interests and, of course, entertain. They can teach children tolerance for other people, customs, and ideas.

Through books, the child who has little access to his grandparents can gain a sensitivity and respect for old people. The child living on a farm can catch a glimpse of what it would be like to live in a high-rise apartment building. The urbanized child can be transported to the village of an early American Indian child. The sheltered child can experience the piognancy and finality of death.

Books help our children to choose their heroes. Marlene Kropf says:

> That's what happened to me. Someone sent me on the way to meet Marian Anderson, the contralto, first in *The Deep River Girl* and later in *My Lord, What a*

Morning. She was a heroic presence in my life for many years. I read everything I could find about her and saved my money to buy her records. Her courage in living and her devotion cast a spell over me[19]

But with so many books to choose from, how can we be sure of making the right choice? We must remember that a poor book will shove a child back a step or two. A mediocre book builds laziness into a child, denying him any challenge at an age when he is best prepared for it. A good book will encourage a creative response from the child, teaching him to think and to use his own original ideas.

A good book for children looks at life with hope. The characters may be in difficulty and crying for help in situations they cannot resolve but they never give way to total hopelessness. Even in their darkest moments children are not totally defeated.[20]

Good children's books must have about them a sense of the wonder of the world. In spite of the difficulties living can present, children still believe that there is "delight and joy and beauty, and something more—a vision of what can be."[21]

There is a sense of adventure in good children's books, a feeling that the unexpected could happen. There is also the sense of being a part of nature, and there is a sympathy for animals and their lives.[22]

A good book respects a child's intelligence, his pride, his dignity, and most of all his individuality and his capacity to grow. It must make the child feel that he is an important part of life.[23]

Lullabies are the earliest literature of childhood. Most of these tunes are uncomplicated and chosen for their simple and melodious charm. The tiny, impressionable baby is already being introduced to listening through these comforting words and tunes before sleep. The older baby is also gaining a sensitivity to word likenesses and differences as he listens to the cadence of pronunciation and correct phrasing from Mother Goose with its rhymes and rhythms.

Looking and listening go hand in hand for the toddler. Large, brightly colored picture books of animals and objects and well-illustrated word books are great for this age. The parent can read the little bit of story tucked into the corner of each picture, but the illustrations explain themselves to the child when he "reads" the book by himself.

I recall a picture book given to our daughter when she was three years old. Although there was very little print on the pages we read it to her again and again. She liked to sit in her little rocking chair and "read" it by herself. Sometime ago, as we cleaned her room together, she picked it up and said, "This is one book I want to keep!"

For new readers the title is important, too. Children usually choose an obvious title rather than one that is too literary or one with a strange name that conveys no meaning.

The print also affects a child's choice. A solid page of type poorly spaced and unbroken by pictures causes the young reader to say, "It's too hard!" before he has read a word.

First and second graders prefer nature stories and easy fairy tales, myths, and legends. They also love Bible stories.

The third grade child is fascinated by the imaginary world but also begins to display an interest in real life, particularly in the life of children in other lands.

Nine-year-olds like to read for information, although they respond to exciting adventure stories, too.

Ten-year-olds like mysteries, tales of magic, animal stories, and biographies of famous people.

In choosing a book for a child, we must give consideration to the content and to the craftsmanship of the author. Does the author portray life as it is or as it can be? Book characters should seem real and consistent with the setting of the story.

Most of us experience some problems from time to time regarding our child's reading. Some children show little interest in books.

Michael had no time for reading because he was building radio sets for all the kids on his block. His mother was concerned. She tried to encourage him to read *Robinson Crusoe* and *Treasure Island* as the other boys were doing. Instead, he spent hours with huge radio books, and his mother strongly suspected that he would never have wanted to learn to read at all if it had not been for explanations under the pictures in his radio books.

If we want practical children such as Michael to enjoy reading, we must approach them through their interests and supply them with reading material they feel is helpful and rewarding.

Additional influences are the parents' reading habits, the conversation in the home, and the number and kinds of books that surround the child. All these play a large part in his interest in reading.

Can a child read too much? Yes. There are children who read books as an escape from their own unhappy situation or surroundings. However, it is not too likely that a child who lives a wholesome life will read too much.

Let us not forget that the Bible is a marvelous piece of literature. Of course, it is more than a book of literature or a book of facts. It is the Word of God and a guide for all of life.

Children are fascinated with Bible stories about real men and women. These stories are full of adventure and excitement. Children respond to God, the Creator. They also respond to Him as a Person who loves, who protects, who cares, and whose presence is with them everywhere anytime. They accept the stories of Jesus Christ.

My husband and I felt it was a privilege, not merely a duty, to acquaint our children with the Bible. When they were very small, I read to them directly from the

Bible. I read in my own way, using familiar words they could understand. Later, Bible storybooks did come into our home. There are many good Bible storybooks on the market today that retell the stories in a way that is understandable to children.

I was warmed while reading *Longer Flight* by Annis Duff to discover how she presented the Bible to her children.[24] Their first introduction to the Bible was by ear. When Mrs. Duff ran out of small talk during the hours of baby-tending, she made conversation by reciting favorite passages from the Bible, such as the Magnificat, a Psalm, or something from Revelations. The Duff children had their first acquaintance with the printed Bible at Christmastime. The little "Bible" was the book, *The Christ Child,* by Maud and Miska Petersham, beautifully illustrated with selected passages.[25]

Books such as *Pilgrim's Progress* fascinate the imaginative mind of a child and subtly teach important truths, too.

Family reading is not only an effective way to guide your family's literary background, but it is a way of learning to know each other better as you share comments and reactions. The whole range of good and bad is covered in the reading hour, and many families have gotten into lively discussions of moral values following the reading of a certain book.

Reading books together provides good family togetherness. An eight-year-old boy once remarked, "I wonder what families do that don't read books together. It's like not knowing each other's friends." Books do seem like friends.

Choose the *best* literature for family reading. Remember that

> My book and heart
> Shall never part . . .

. . . and that great books mold great lives.

9

The Child Learns Self-Esteem

Three preschoolers were at play. For a time they shared with a great deal of common interest and enthusiasm. Then two went off and played by themselves, ignoring the third playmate. Before long the forsaken one cried out, "I'm here! I'm here! Don't you see I'm here?" The lad was expressing a need which is universal. He wanted to be noticed and recognized as a person of worth. [26]

The great plague of inferiority feelings starts early in life. A person who feels worthless and does not like himself will contribute little to life. To have a sense of significance, the individual person must be noticed and appreciated and loved for what he is. There is no better way of giving the child a sense of his personal worth.

Judge Philip Gilliam says, "The lack of affection between father and mother is the greatest cause of delinquency I know." [27] When parents spend special time and effort cultivating their friendship as husband and wife, they not only enrich their lives together but they are also enriching their children's lives.

A mother said, "My four-year-old daughter watched me give her baby brother his morning bath. I gently patted him dry playfully dressed him, and firmly but lovingly held him close as I fed him. My daughter asked, 'Mommy, do you love me as much as you love baby brother?'

" 'Why of course, dear!' I exclaimed. 'I love you just as much as I love your brother.'

" 'But, Mommy,' her voice quivered, 'Why don't you love me with your hands the way you love baby brother?' "

All children crave a love that is demonstrated. "To love with our hands—to cuddle, to hold on the knee, to take a small hand into ours, or to put an arm around the shoulder as Jesus did—takes time, but how much we would benefit from such intimate closeness with each other." [28]

It's important for a mother to spend some time alone with each child every day simply for the pleasure of his company. More important than words, it is a way of saying " 'You rate with me. Right now you are more important to me than anything or anybody else in the world!' It is a way of building self-confidence into the child, which is so necessary if he is to succeed in life." [29]

Psychiatrist James Dobson suggests that parents examine their attitudes toward their child. He asks, "Are you secretly disappointed that your child is so ordinary? Have you rejected him, at times, because of his lack of appeal and charm? . . . Quite obviously, you can't teach a child to respect himself when you dislike him for reasons of your own."[30]

Counselors hear a lot about the moments of pain or loneliness that parents can cause their children: "I would be gone for hours as a child, and nobody noticed." "I felt like I was a burden to my parents." "I was appreciated only when I was good." Such memories hurt and eat away at adult self-confidence.

> One deeply inhibited father, twice divorced and lonely, broke into deep sobs during a psychodrama experience as he relived his childhood experiences with report cards. "I brought home D's and F's for years, and Dad looked from his cabinet work long enough to say, 'Have your mom sign it.' I was never beaten or mistreated physically, but nobody cared if I failed."[31]

A good home has been defined as "a place where a child can bring a bad report card." The bad report card needs to be accepted, but an understanding parent will seek for the causes. The child needs to be given enough pressure to challenge him but not enough to make him discouraged.

Dr. Joseph Bobbitt, a well-known child psychologist, commented:

> There have been studies showing that the child who has the lowest self-esteem is the one who isn't permitted

to say anything at the dinner table. The one with the next lowest image of himself is the child who is allowed to dominate conversation. Highest on the list is the youngster whose parents tell him, "Yes, you can speak up—when it's your turn." That statement reveals the important balance between love and control which produces emotionally secure and healthy children.[32]

Dr. Haim G. Ginott writes about a code of communication that he calls "childrenese." It's based on respect and skill. The messages must preserve both the child's and the parent's self-respect. Furthermore, a statement of understanding needs to precede advice or instruction. "Such responses," says Dr. Ginott, "create intimacy between parent and child. When the child feels understood, his loneliness and hurt diminish because they are understood, and his love for his mother is deepened because she understands. Mother's sympathy serves as an emotional band-aid for the bruised ego."[33]

Eric was angry because it rained and the family couldn't go on a picnic. His mother could have said, "There's no use crying about canceled picnics; there'll be another day." But instead, his mother thought for a moment, aware that every child is entitled to his emotions. Eric was showing his disappointment by his anger. She could best help him by showing understanding and respect for his feelings. Soon Eric was able to say, "Oh, well, there'll be another day."

A child's strong feelings don't disappear by telling them to. They do lose their intensity when the listener accepts them and expresses sympathy and understanding.

Dr. Ginott warns that the right time to teach an offender about his personality is not when things go wrong. When mishaps occur, it is best to deal with the event, not with the person. In constructive criticism you point out how to do what has to be done and refrain from making negative remarks about the child's personality.

Sarcasm and cutting cliches only insult the child and give him a feeling of inferiority. The Bible states that the law of kindness should be on the tongue of the woman who loves God. Too often parents react to minor mishaps, such as a broken egg, as though it were a broken leg. Or to a shattered window as though it were a shattered heart. Minor mishaps should be treated as such with children.

When Martin spilled some milk on the table, his mother commented calmly, "I see the milk is spilled. Here is another glass of milk and here is a sponge." Martin cleaned up the table while his mother helped him. She didn't add cutting comments or useless advice. She was tempted to remind him, "Be more careful." But when she saw how grateful he was for her kind silence, she said nothing.

Words of praise should give the child a realistic picture of his accomplishments, not an untrue image of his personality. Kenny helped his father to fix up the base-ment. In the process, he had to move heavy furniture. When his father remarked that it was heavy and hard to move, Kenny was proud that he had done it. Had the father commented that he was very strong, Kenny may have protested, thinking of some stronger boys.

A child needs to be made to feel that he can do something good. Realistic, positive statements help him to develop self-acceptance and form a positive or good opinion of himself, of others, and of the world around him.

Someone had stated, "If a child lives with praise, he learns to appreciate." Perhaps this is one reason why God advises us to be filled with praise—in everything.

10

The Child's Spiritual Development

You say, "God is love." Has your child encountered true love? You say, "God forgives sins." Do you forgive your child? You say, "God does not accept evil." Do you confess your own wrongdoing?

The kind of person you are and the way you handle your child portrays to him his image of God. In countless small ways you are conditioning your child either for or against love, forgiveness, and God's ideals.

The greatest choice a child will ever make is his decision for God in Jesus Christ. The better a child knows what God is like the more decisive will be his choice.

Spiritual development begins in the home. To be sure, we need the Sunday school and the church, but only as supplements. Too many people think of home as a supplement to the church. That's so wrong! It must be reversed if our children are to have proper spiritual direction.

God knew the effectiveness of parental instruction.

Before children go to school is the time to start teaching them about God and His truths and memorizing Scripture with them. You can teach when you tie their shoes, when you comb their hair, and when you work or play together.

Informal teaching during the day is the most effective. Everything we say, how we say it, our attitudes, everything we do, or leave undone—all are visual-aid teaching. Such teaching either illustrates and confirms the verses we teach, or it negates them.

And so the child learns about God. He learns God's ideals, he learns what is right, true, and good by what parents are and what they do:

When they return the extra change at the store.

When they show disapproval of the unfair way a member of a minority or racial group is treated.

When they cheerfully share the work at home.

When they engage in recreation that is wholesome.

When they practice clean habits of speech and conduct.

When they speak respectfully of others.

When they help someone in trouble.

When they talk wisely of money matters.

When they admit their mistakes and ask for forgiveness.

When they attend church faithfully and naturally.

When they talk and act as though God were a person to them, and the new life in Christ a real experience.

The child also grows spiritually when parents associate God with life around them—the beauties of nature, a sunset or sunrise, signs of spring, joyous times as well as difficulties, sorrow or death.

A young mother shared:

> I discovered through my mother's faith and devotion that God was interested in the smallest details of my life. I grew up knowing that the mint tea growing along the roadside which we discovered on a country hike was one of those delightful surprises God has in store. God cared about whether the pattern to a dress was cut out correctly and was aware when the bread flopped. He loved crabby Mr. Rice who lived next door and had compassion on the tiny kitten with the sore eyes. We thanked God for the early blooming crocus and reminded Him that our garden needed rain.

Children are constantly being confronted with heroes of questionable values—perhaps through TV or movies. Christian parents need to acquaint their children with godly heroes by filling their lives with the tales of biblical saints and stories of great Christians both past and contemporary. Reading bedtime stories is a beautiful way of sharing spiritual truths.

> The father of a six-year-old says, "Those Old Testament stories are absolutely fantastic! You can't find more exciting stories anywhere to tell to your kids."

Because of that enthusiasm his son may grow up having more respect for Moses or David than for Superman. At least Moses and David will be strong competitors![34]

Parents can reinforce what the child is learning by taking his Sunday school and Bible school materials and relating them to the week's activities. I was amazed when one mother told me that her child at five years knew many Scripture passages, including Luke 2:1-20 and entire Psalms. She and her husband planned Bible reading and regular prayer periods with their children. They taught their children diligently with plan and purpose.

In the Old Testament, God instructed His children, "And thou shalt love the Lord thy God with all thine heart, and with all thy soul, and with all thy might."

Again He said, "And these words, which I command thee . . . shall be in thine heart:

"And thou shalt teach them diligently unto thy children, and shalt talk of them when thou sittest in thine house, and when thou walkest by the way, and when thou liest down, and when thou risest up" (Deuteronomy 6:5-7).

Of course God didn't expect us to be repeating Bible passages all day long, but He did know that informal teaching during the everyday activities would be most effective.

When the Hebrew child asked why his parents were serving Jehovah and why Jehovah required them to behave in a certain way, his parents would respond by telling their child of the events of grace in which God had acted in their lives.

> The name scholars give to the recitation of God's mighty acts is the "credo." Perhaps each family ought to have its own credo, or story of the acts of God in the life of the family, to retell when questions come up about why we live as we do. . . . This would help children to learn to recognize acts of God in their own lives which call for response in terms of faith and obedience. [35]

Instead of the perfunctory rhyming table grace, one family with small children substitutes the question, "What do you want to thank God for?" The child usually wants to thank God for the people that she sees sitting around the table, for some favorite food that she sees, or for some especially good time that she had during the day. [36]

When travelling, another family with small children sings, "Little children, praise the Lord," substituting, "Praise Him for our blue van," "our yellow house, " or whatever they can think of that they especially appreciate that day. [37]

The child forms his own opinions. He'll likely compare God to you—his parents. Your goal is to expose him to God and Jesus Christ, and to share together as he discovers God—the ultimate authority in life.

Later on in his spiritual development, he will have to

accept these truths as his own. He either accepts the Bible as truth, or rejects it. He either accepts Jesus Christ as His personal Savior from sin and guilt, or rejects Him and flounders about in self-sufficiency and in false security. Yes, he makes his decisions, but you are available and can help him to understand God and His ideas and how God works in his own little world —in his own life, among friends, schoolmates, and in the community.

Choosing Christ is not a matter of memorizing doctrines or merely abiding by certain codes of behavior. A turning to Christ is rooted in the deep choices of the heart. We can trust God to work with His child at His own speed.

You continue daily to bring your child to God. And if he refuses to accept God? Parents continue to pray. We know he can never shake off those early impressions and truths. By faith we claim the promise, " . . . believe on the Lord Jesus Christ, and thou shalt be saved, and thy house" (Acts 16:31).

God's grace and love are available for anyone, whenever he or she believes on Him and follows Him— whether or not Christian training was a part of that person's life. However, from the Bible and from history we clearly see the results of a godly heritage. A child can never forget such teaching. He may ignore it, or deny it, but it follows him through life. (*See* Proverb 22:6.)

"We can't experience God for our children, but we

can share our experiences of God with them and help them recognize God's activity in their own lives."[38]

11

Guard Your Child's Health

Years ago a wise man said, "Tell me what you eat and I will tell you what you are."

Diet does play an important role in shaping our personalities by helping to control how we feel, look, and react. Lack of certain nutrients may account for nervousness, grouchiness, fatigue, depression, and a lack of concentration. Of course, food can't prevent and cure all these disorders, but by serving the food the body requires we can contribute toward sound health for our children.

It was Thomas Edison, the inventive genius, who said, "I keep my health by dieting; people eat too much and drink too much. Eating has become a habit with almost everyone; it is like taking morphine—the more you take the more you want. People gorge themselves with rich food. They use up their time and ruin their digestion and poison themselves.

"If the doctors would prescribe diet instead of drugs," he added, "the ailments of normal man would disappear. Half the people are food-drunk all the time. Diet is the secret of my health. I always live abstemiously. It is a religion with me!" Perhaps this discipline he gave his body contributed to his mental capacity for great discoveries and inventions.

In a booklet produced by the National Dairy Council of Chicago we are reminded that we need food for three functions:

1. To build and repair tissues, bones, muscles, nerves, blood, all vital organs, fingernails, skin, and hair.
2. To regulate body processes and to keep the body working at its best.
3. To supply energy for every conscious and unconscious action.

Proteins, minerals, vitamins, fats, carbohydrates, and water are the substances in food that perform these three tasks.

The child very early develops a "sweet tooth." The main objection to foods such as cookies, candy, and rich crackers and pastries is that they are largely composed of refined starch, sugar, and fat. They will quickly satisfy a child's appetite because they are rich in calories, but they are comparatively devoid of vitamins, minerals, and other essential factors. "They cheat a child by making him feel well fed when he is being partly starved and by spoiling his appetite for better foods."[39]

One mother said that when she stopped buying snack

foods, she discovered that the same amount of money used for snacks would go as far or farther in buying high-nutrition foods.[40]

Children do occasionally need to nibble between meals, but give them something with food value. Apples are full of carbohydrates, valuable minerals, and vitamins. Citrus fruits help to keep the saliva in the mouth neutral, rather than acid, so they are friends of your child's teeth. They are also low in calories but high in vitamin C. A glass of milk and two tablespoons of peanut butter in a sandwich give high quality protein. Nutritionists say this compares to three ounces of steak. Carrot sticks and crisp celery in a bowl of ice water make a tempting snack. The body burns up more energy in digesting raw vegetables than it obtains from them so actually they are slimming foods. Some nutritionists suggest drinking water instead of soft drinks. It's less fattening and a lot more economical!

As a family, we've been grateful to God for our good health, and I believe the type of foods we eat has contributed much. Through the years, I've served simply prepared, nourishing foods and familiar dishes because they are cheaper, quicker, easier, and healthier than fancy, expensive, rich foods! We eat some old-fashioned foods like bean soup, cornmeal mush, milk puddings, and mostly fruit for dessert. We frequently substitute honey for sugar. We appreciate dairy products.

With the rising cost of living, don't begin cutting out nutritious food. A balanced diet of milk and milk products, protein food, fruit, and vegetables is a must for you and your family for health's sake. Plant protein can be combined with meat in your diet to enable you to get the necessary amont of protein without needing expensive meats or protein supplements.

Cheerful, matter-of-fact parents eating with children make eating more pleasant. Perhaps it isn't possible to eat together at every meal, but aim for at least *one* meal a day together.

One of the ten "Beatitudes for Homemakers" reads: "Blessed is she who serves laughter and smiles with every meal; for her cheerfulness is an aid to mental and physical digestion."[41]

Remember, too, that favorite foods make eating fun. Within each group of foods needed for health is a wide choice. A child's likes and dislikes sometimes change without warning, but having to eat at least one spoonful of everything you serve helps him gradually to outgrow his notions. Give him small servings. Let him tell you when he wants second helpings. Allow a child sufficient time to eat a meal.

At our house what a rewarding experience it was to prepare at the request of the children foods they ate only with encouragement several years before.

The child who is fed a nutritious diet will have lots of energy. Activity outdoors allows children fresh oxygen intake, and the direct rays of sunshine provide vitamin D. Today many children do not have access to a backyard, a meadow, or a woods, but every mother can take her child for a walk or run on the sidewalk or to a park playground. She can allow some space in the house for rough play at certain hours of the day.

Dr. Charles W. Hertzler, a local doctor, says that there is less sickness when there are more activities outdoors. Physical fitness should be a part of childhood. The purpose of physical fitness is to have a healthy heart, and with it a healthy body and mind. Exercises such as walking, running, biking, swimming, and playing ball are *essential* for physical fitness.

One year our boys hopped onto the school bus right in front of our home and then off again in the evening. During the cold winter months, the teachers seldom let them play outdoors. We had no outside chores for them at home. That winter they caught cold after cold. Then we moved into a new setup. Here they had outside chores and a paper route. Their colds decreased amazingly. In fact, that winter they were the only ones in our family to escape the Asian flu.

"Children don't have legs anymore," growl school authorities. Walking involves all the body muscles and is an excellent exercise for the whole family. Whether in the city or in the country, a mother can set aside an hour to refresh herself by taking a brisk walk with her children.

Good eating and exercising habits are not enough for the healthy child. The active child needs a rest time for his body to catch up. Some children burn up more energy than others and need more rest and sleep to build up their bodies. One of my sons did not nap after three years of age and slept fewer hours at night than his brother who napped until an older age. You'll need to determine how much your child needs.

The preschooler usually takes a nap daily, or he may have a regular quiet period when he relaxes and looks at pictures or books, or colors, or listens to records. If this habit is established early in life, it will be much easier to follow later on. A certain nap-time routine directly after lunch, before he can get involved in other activities, will make it easier to establish this habit.

Make sure that your child's hands and face are clean and that he has had a drink and used the toilet before his nap. If he is a toddler, his diapers should be dry and secure. Take off his shoes and see that his clothing is loose and comfortable. Perhaps you could tell a story or sing a song. Tuck him in with a kiss and a hug. Sleep requires a relaxed body and mind.

A child might resist sleep at nighttime because this is the only time of day he sees his father. Or perhaps he is involved in an exciting play activity or watching an interesting TV show. He has to go to a room all by himself, leaving behind the entertainment and action and the people he loves. Or he may have heard something scary and disturbing. Perhaps he inwardly resents the absence of a parent. We should try to discover why the child resists sleep and then help him to resolve his fears and find security. In the words of Dr. Flanders

Dunbar, "A sleepless child makes a restless, awkward adolescent and a tired or anxious adult."

Children respect their parents when they are fair and firm. You can't force your child to sleep, but you can soothe him and accustom his body to the habit of regular, early bedtime. It is a good idea to prepare the child ahead of time. Tell him that it will be bedtime as soon as he has finished the game or activity he is doing. Don't plan any stimulating activity for this time. Bedtime can become a happy event with a special game, songs, or stories reserved only for this time.

When the child ends his action day close to his parents' heart and arms, and with the assurance of God's love, he is prepared for a pleasant, relaxing journey into dreamland.

Your child's body cannot be replaced. It's priceless. God wants it for the dwelling place of His Spirit. Help your son and daughter to develop good health habits and take good care of their bodies.

12

Make Home a Safe Place

Is your home a safe place for your child?

Look around and see. Perhaps you may discover some interesting facts, as did the father in the following experience:

One father, a safety engineer, volunteered to baby-sit with his eighteen-month-old son for an afternoon and received an accelerated course in environmental safety. After first rescuing Bobby from under the table lamp he had pulled to the floor by yanking on the cord, Dad then discovered him nearly headfirst in the toilet. Later Bobby was found poking a metal pencil into an electric outlet. Soon a little cry from the bedroom brought Dad running to find the little one sitting among the contents of the sewing basket, holding up a pricked finger.

When Father made a trip to the basement and forgot to close the door, he found Bobby ready to make a dive down the basement stairs. Before the afternoon ended aspirin, turpentine, and weed killer were taken from Bobby, and he was rescued from a perch halfway up a ladder. Dad wrote an essay entitled "How Do They Live

So Long?" for the National Safety Council, following his busy afternoon![42]

The tiny infant is often more active than we realize. Unless a safety belt is used, he should never be left alone on the Bathinette. No baby at any age should be left unattended on a table or a bed. Babies two or three days old are able to wriggle far enough to fall.

The mattress should be a tight fit in his crib so that the baby's head does not get wedged in the side. It is best to use a tightly secured bumper pad so that his head or legs will not get caught in the crib bars. Do not use thin, loose plastic to waterproof his crib mattress. Be alert that he does not get his face buried in his blankets.

The climbing baby is at a dangerous age. If parents worry and become overprotective in an effort to try to prevent all accidents, they only succeed in making a child dependent and fearful. On the other hand, if they are aware of the common dangers and use common sense in avoiding them, most serious accidents can be prevented.

The toddler's high chair should have a broad base to prevent it from tipping, a harness to secure the child, and a latch to keep the tray from being removed. The climbing baby needs to be harnessed when taking a ride in his stroller or baby carriage. Keep furniture far enough from the window to prevent the baby from climbing up on the sill. Window screens are too flimsy to be a safeguard against a child's falling. Upstairs windows should be opened only from the top, or have guards. Until the child can handle himself safely on steps, there should be a gate at the top and sometimes at the bottom of the stairway.

The young, exploring child should never be left alone in the bathtub or the bathroom. He should never play unsupervised near a washing machine or wringer that is in operation. Children sometimes climb into clothes dryers, so you should know where your child is before turning the dial.

"If after a fall on the head, a baby stops crying within fifteen minutes, keeps a good color and doesn't vomit, there is little chance that he has injured his brain. He can be allowed to resume his normal life right a-way."[43] However, serious intracranial hemorrhage can show up five or six hours later and is accompanied by a fixed, dilated pupil on the side of the injury. Usually there is a brief period of unconsciousness at the time of the injury. So should your child suffer a severe blow to the head and suspicious symptoms develop, get in touch with your doctor.

A most dangerous time of the day for the small child is when his mother is preparing meals. Because of the risk of spattering grease or of tripping and spilling something hot on children, it is best to have a designated play area away from the mother's feet. Wear short or close-fitting sleeves when cooking and use pot holders instead of apron corners or dish towels when lifting hot utensils from the stove. Pot handles should always be turned to the back of the stove because even a baby can reach a surprising distance when he tries. The mother should never cook with a baby in her arms. Hot food or drink should never be passed over the body of a child. When you are serving the meal, put hot containers in the middle of the table. Tablecloths that can be pulled and bring dishes crashing down on the head of the child should not be used.

In case of an accident in which the child does get burned, immediately plunge the burned area into cold water, or even cold milk if that is more convenient. You can add ice to the water and keep the burn submerged until the pain lets up. If you run cold tap water over the burned area, take care that the water pressure doesn't break or injure the skin.

Child poisonings also take place most frequently when the mother is preoccupied in preparing meals. The preschooler is bored and hungry and decides to explore the forbidden cupboards. An older child can be a great help at these busy times by entertaining the younger ones. Or perhaps the mother can occupy the three- to five-year-old by letting him carry unbreakable items to the table. She can have special coloring books or some other activity that she pulls out only at this time.

Children at the exploring, tasting age will eat almost anything, no matter how it tastes. They love good-tasting medicines, cigarettes, matches, and even chomp on electric cords.

Dr. Spock has listed the substances that most frequently cause dangerous poisoning in children:

1. Aspirin and other drugs.
2. Insect and rat poisons.
3. Kerosene, gasoline, benzene and cleaning fluids.
4. Lead in paint that a child has chewed off something. (Most indoor paint and toy paint contains no lead. The danger is from outdoor paint on windowsills, porches, etc., and from outdoor paint that has been used at home to repaint toys, cribs, and other furniture.)
5. Liquid furniture and auto polish.
6. Lye, alkalis used for cleaning drains, bowls, ovens.
7. Oil of wintergreen
8. Plant sprays. [44]

Find inaccessible places in the kitchen, bathroom, utility room, and basement or garage for any household products that contain toxic ingredients. Unused and outdated medicines should be discarded twice a year. Internal medicines should be stored separately from external ones. Adaptable latches and locks can be used for cupboards and cabinets. Matches should be kept in high places that are impossible for determined young climbers to reach.

In case of poisoning, call your doctor immediately and tell him what the suspected poison is. If the poison is a petroleum product, do not induce vomiting because these products are most harmful when breathed or choked into the lungs. Vomiting can cause the throat to be burned again if the poison swallowed is an acid or caustic cleanser. A child who is having a convulsion should not be induced to vomit.[45]

Some pediatricians recommend having a bottle of ipecac in your medicine cabinet to induce vomiting to empty the child's stomach immediately in case of swallowing some other type of poison. You can also give the child egg white, cream, or tepid water. Rush the child to the doctor for further treatment and be sure to take the bottle that contained the poison or drug along with you to assist the doctor in making his diagnosis for treatment.

Charts of common poisons with their antidotes are available from your hospital emergency center. It is a good idea to keep these tacked in some easily accessible place in case they are needed.

The crawling child who still puts things into his mouth should be protected from small objects such as beads, marbles, buttons, peas, screws, small pieces of a tinker toy set, coins, pins, needles, safety pins, and so on. He should never be given nuts or popcorn to eat. He might breathe these small objects into his windpipe, which could cause choking. If he does have a choking accident, hold him upside down and slap him vigorously between the shoulder blades. If he keeps on choking, rush him to the nearest hospital or doctor's office. Don't wait for anything. Let someone else phone ahead.

Sometimes children stuff small objects into their ears or noses. With the aid of a tweezers you might be able to grasp a soft object that isn't too far in. If the child is old enough to understand, have him blow his nose. If the object is smooth and hard, allow the doctor to go after it; you would be almost certain to push it in farther. A bad-smelling discharge tinged with blood from your child's nose may mean that a small foreign object is lodged there.

A doctor remarked that he can't count the times he is called to the emergency room to care for an accident because a child was playing on the street. He said, "Sometimes we are lucky and can mend the broken body, but too often we can't." Do not operate your car without first knowing where your child is. Neither is the family car a plaything. When the car is parked, make sure that the windows are closed and the doors are locked so that your children cannot play in it.

The yard should be a safe place to play in. Keep the rubbish and trash in containers. Sharp tools should not be allowed to lie around. Place the hedge clippers, ax, and saw out of the child's reach.

Small children should never be allowed near a rotary lawn mower. There are two kinds of danger from a rotary mower. The first and most obvious danger is from the whirling blades, which can cut feet and hands as well as grass. The second and less obvious danger is that the blades can pick up an object and hurl it with terrific force. These objects can bruise and cut as well as put out a person's eyes.

The watchword for mothers is "think ahead of time." We can trust God to keep His protecting hand on our homes, but this does not license us to be careless and unconcerned. Between you and your child's guardian angel you may be able to save your small one from a needless accident.

13

Caring for the Sick Child

The home I entered that afternoon was cluttered. The ironing lay untouched. The breakfast dishes were stacked in the sink. The mother apologized, but she really didn't need to. She had spent the day making a stuffed rag toy for her sick child. She had moved her small son's bed into the room where she was working, so that he could watch her. Love, she believes, is an excellent cure!

Someone has said that part of a mother's role is safekeeper of the family's health for children and adults. Even with the best of preventive care and to-day's advanced medical science, illness is still a part of life.

The mother of young children needs a sixth sense. Is Freddie really ill, or does his tummy ache because he doesn't like his breakfast? Sally, too, may feel shooting pains when it is her turn to do the dishes. But what if the child is really ill, the mother worries after sending her child off to school? What if the school nurse calls? Or what if the mother hears after getting home from work that the child was in bed all day at school?

A doctor friend advises that the best time to decide if a child has recovered enough to go to school is the night before. In the morning is a poor time to make the decision because after a night's sleep the child may feel better only to get worse as the day progresses.

Childhood diseases are easy to recognize after the swollen glands or spots appear, but a lot of symptoms are more elusive. Observe the child's color. Is it pale or flushed, or is there a bluish tinge to the skin or finger-nails? Are there any swellings or rashes? Is his breath sour? Does he have fever or abnormal body functions? Has his weight suddenly shifted? The child who is old enough to talk can tell you where there is pain, itching, or tenderness. If you call the doctor, carefully report these observations, as they will aid him greatly in mak-ing his diagnosis.

A fretful baby may tend to bury one ear in the mat-tress or pull on it as he cries and tosses in his crib. This might indicate an earache.

The mother of a football player noticed one evening that her son was behaving in a sluggish manner. He didn't want to talk about the terrible headache he had had since colliding with another player. His mother noticed that the pupil in one eye was very tiny. She immediately took him to his doctor who discovered a brain concussion.

There are simple home remedies that can be used at the first sign of certain types of illnesses. For fever, pain or colds, give aspirin, plenty of liquids, and rest. In my home we start sucking a lemon at the first signs of a sniffle, sore throat, or virus. We also use a simple cough syrup made of equal parts of lemon juice, honey, olive oil, and glycerine. For an upset stomach or loose bowels, give hot tea, a bland diet, or an accepted remedy that the doctor has approved of and you have on hand. Watch the child carefully, however; if he doesn't respond positively, contact your family doctor.

Sometimes giving medicine to the young child results in a struggle. Here are some suggestions to improve the pill-pushing routine.

1. Slightly raise the child's head. If he remains lying flat on his back, the medicine may go down the windpipe instead of into his stomach.

2. Let him know that you are giving medicine even when you put it in food. At our house we hurdled pill-taking time by crushing the pill and serving it in a teaspoon of honey.

3. If your child refuses his medicine, try again.

4. Don't call medicine "candy." Your child might like it so much he'll take it on his own when you aren't looking.

5. Give only the medicine prescribed specifically for this child for this illness by his doctor. Every medicine is a complicated drug.

6. Read the lable before giving, to avoid mistakes.

7. Keep medicines out of children's reach.

8. Never give a small tablet, such as a baby aspirin,

to a small child. It should first be dissolved in a little water.

One of the most unpleasant features of being sick is the feeling of isolation. Remind yourself that you are your child's best nurse. Your familiar touch contains more comfort than the most highly trained hands. You know best what lights the spark of interest in his eyes, what tickles his funny bone, and the kind of back rub he appreciates. Live one hour at a time as you share yourself with him. There will be time for your other duties later.

Extra loving when a child is feeling low is like an icing on a cake, which is sweet in the eating and a good source of extra energy. Rocking, holding, cuddling, and loving the sick baby or toddler are powerful factors in his recovery.

Children consider rest an unreasonable restriction even when they are sick. Quiet play for the older toddler or the preschool-age child in his high chair or on the living-room sofa is acceptable. Depending on how contagious his illness is, an older child can assist you in entertaining him. Play games and sing together. Read his favorite books and Bible stories. Relate them to familiar experiences and needs.

Several days' stay in bed will be more pleasant for the older child patient and more convenient for you if you brighten up the sickroom a bit. Colorful curtains, interesting pictures, a fish bowl, or pretty flowers make a room pleasant and attractive.

A bed table can be made by folding two legs of a card table and propping that side on the bed with a pillow or several books. Prop up your patient by putting an upside-down chair behind his back. Place a piece of heavy plastic under the sheet to save worry from spilling accidents. Work out a bell signal in which he rings once if he wants a drink of water and twice if it's the bathroom. To keep things tidy, pin an open paper bag to the side of the mattress for waste paper and tissues. See that there is a clock in the room.

Contentment, cheerfulness, and laughter are effective medicines. One mother makes a treasure chest that is usually successful. She collects everything odd and spare, from last year's Christmas greetings to her husband's old watch to the sea shells she gathered at the ocean, and places them in a box. Sorting through such "treasures" can entertain and amuse the imaginative child.

Give the sick child old magazines, mail-order catalogs, blunt scissors, paste, and paper to make scrapbooks. Or pin the pictures he cuts out on the curtains or walls. Let him sort buttons from the button jar. He may be delighted with the photograph album, a magnet, a magnifying glass, a mirror, a box of clay, or well-selected TV shows.

A record player and lots of children's records helped to entertain our youngsters. Even the three-year-old literally spent hours listening to and memorizing the songs as she recovered from chicken pox and mumps.

Call the teacher for the school child's assignments and consider yourself the teacher's proxy for the duration of the illness. Unless the disease is contagious, let friends come for visits after school hours.

Sickness does come to every home. We can grumble and complain, making everyone unhappy, or we can cheerfully accept this illness and inconvenience, knowing that God cares and loves. He can turn what could have been a miserable day into a blessing.

ON HOLDING A SICK CHILD

Somehow this circle of my arms allowed for rest
And such firm pressure of my chin upon your hair
Said love was there. So now you sleep.
But all the while my thoughts escape
The room, wandering distressed across the sum
Of what I'd planned so carefully and now
Will not be finished or, perhaps, begun.

Then I recall myself as child, who could
Not fathom (when disease or pain oppressed)
How anything or anyone could matter more
Than what my loneliness desired or missed:
How simply someone being near quieted fear.

Now as I hold you closer than I ought
There is another also caught with the embrace—
A distant youngster, thin, and long forgotten,
Long alone . . . wearing my face.[46]

CHARLES A. WAUGAMAN

14

The Child Faces Death

Grandfather carefully peeled the peach firmly held in his wrinkled hand. Even now, eighty-one years old, he wouldn't be caught loafing. His four-year-old granddaughter, Sue, loved every minute of his stay. They frolicked, teased, and enjoyed each other. She too was peeling peaches.

Suddenly her childish voice broke the silence, "Grandpa, aren't you glad you'll soon go to heaven?"

Grandfather paused, his gaze suddenly seemed far away, "Yes, honey, I'm glad it won't be long."

Grandfather's visit soon ended. Four months later Sue accompanied her mother to a distant state where Grandfather was now hospitalized. As she entered the hospital room, Sue walked boldly to his bedside and placed her little hand in Grandfather's outstretched white hand. "Hello, honey," his voice quivered, "I guess I'll soon be in heaven." During the following thirty minutes they recalled their happy times together.

A month later when Sue was told of Grandfather's death, she exclaimed, "Now he isn't sick anymore. He's having a good time with Jesus. Mother, when will I go to heaven?"

Sue's parents had faith in the One who promised, "In my Father's house are many mansions . . . I go to prepare a place for you. . . . that where I am ye may be also" (John 14:2,3). Sue had absorbed their wholesome attitudes.

As we involve children in natural, normal circumstances leading up to death, they learn to accept it as a part of life. Lois brought her elderly mother home from the hospital to spend her last days. She placed her in her old-fashioned mahogany bed beside the window where she could enjoy the fleecy clouds, the rustling, swaying leaves and branches, the geese in the pond, and the children's frolics on the lawn.

The children carried trays to her regularly. They shared their school achievements with her. Grandma's wit and alertness brightened their visits to her room. They questioned her about her illness, about death, and about life after death. They expressed their love and affection in many little ways.

Visitors were encouraged to "admit that it's farewell," as they came from near and far. They sat beside her and reminisced about happy days of the past. They shared their bouquets while she was alive by voicing their appreciation and their love and admiration for her. They also conversed about life and death, about heaven and eternity, and about the center of glory, Jesus Christ.

It wasn't long until Grandma gave her last look of warm love and gratitude. To be sure, Grandma's death was an emotional strain with sorrow and sadness, but it was also a precious and enriching experience for Lois's children.

Death does not always come only to the old. One mother's five-year-old son, David, lost his playmate owing to complications following measles. Hurt and puzzled, David asked questions but resented any offers of sympathy. Sometime later while visiting in the dead child's home, David said sadly, "If you were here now, Ephraim, I'd let you ride my bike."

"I'll bet you would," David's mother replied, "and the two of you would have lots of fun." Then she reminded him that he had loaned his favorite toy car to Ephraim when he was sick. "Did you know that Ephraim was holding on tight to it when he died?" she asked. After that David could cry, and it seemed that the wound began to heal.[47]

A young mother shared from her experience with her two young sons when her thirty-year-old husband suddenly died. She felt that her boys' adjustment was partly related to the time she spent alone with them immediately following the death of their father. Together she and her sons had had a memorable time of sharing, crying, and holding each other physically in supportive arms. They talked about their life with the father, placing in their minds the reality "that his body was too sick to live here." She allowed her sons to work out their grief in useful ways by helping to pack their father's things. [48]

In contrast to these experiences, when Linda's favorite aunt became gravely ill, Linda was shielded from all reality. She was denied the privilege of sharing this deep emotional experience with her family. Linda's parents refused to take her to see her aunt in her aunt's last days because they were afraid that the ghastly facial appearance would frighten their child.

They deceived Linda on her aunt's death saying, "Aunty has taken a trip and won't return for a long time." They even invented actual accounts of her stay in another state. Linda's parents decided to wait until Linda learned about death before they would reveal Aunty's absence.

One of the most difficult problems for a modern parent is that of being able to help his child meet the hard places in such a way that he will grow stronger by having lived through them. Perhaps the most dreaded of these hard places is the child's first encounter with the death of a person he loves.

Before the parent can help his child he, himself, must come to grips with death. Jesus Christ promised us, "Because I live, you shall live also." What a hope and thrill to know that some day Christ will communicate with us face to face!

Of course death brings physical separation and sorrow, but our sorrow is an expression of our own hurt and not hopeless grief for the one who has made his peace with God before death.

When my heavenly Father beckons me to come home, I want my funeral service to be joyous. I want the entire congregation to rise and to join in that great triumphant Hallelujah Anthem!

When your child asks, "What is death?" you can explain, "It is the separation of that part of me that says 'I' from the part of me that was my body. The body that is dead will be buried and will decay. The 'me' that will never die is released from its earthly house and goes to live with God."

When the child questions, "What makes people die?" you can explain that the heart stops beating and with no more fresh blood to replenish the poisoned blood, the body can't function. You can also explain that God does control a life span and when the individual has finished it, it is time to move on. This can be compared to growth from one phase into another or to a change of jobs.

When the child asks, "Where do they go?" the parent with a trusting faith in God can give a clear-cut answer. The parent can use this with the older child as a springboard to sharing the truth of Resurrection, the changing of the physical body to the spiritual. This life is the cocoon stage. Then one day comes the brilliant transformation like a colorful, winged butterfly—a life utterly different with absence of fear, pain, sorrow, sickness, tension, and death.

Loman sat on the bed with his legs crossed beneath him. Piled high around him were games, books, and records. He reached for his crayons and started coloring. "Mother," he began without lifting his eyes from the picture, "when can I go with Jesus? He told me yesterday that He wants me to come."

His mother mustered her courage. After nearly a year's battle with her son's leukemia, her reserve was low. She took his pale, thin hand in hers, "Honey, I don't know when. Do you really want to go?"

Loman continued, "I love you and Daddy and everybody. But with Jesus I won't have that old needle or my sore legs, and I won't have to go back to the hospital." He put aside his colors and lay limply on the bed. The flash of energy was gone.

Loman's parents had prepared him to face death, for they were not afraid.

15

The Special Child

Born as a hydrocephalic without sight or hearing or any human potential, Maria was given only several months to live by the doctors. Maria had stumps in place of legs or feet. A tumor the size of a head grew on her back. Only the little arms and hands were formed perfectly. But who would care for her even for a few months?

A day-nursery run by the Sisters of Mercy accepted Maria. To still her constant crying, they carried her everywhere they went. Six months passed. Maria gave no hint of awareness. Then one day the unbelievable happened. Maria smiled. Gradually one talent after another developed in the baby who had no potential. After many more months Maria spoke her first word, "light"!

To the Sisters there could have been no better word. With it came light from God that they should have the tumor removed. The surgeon hesitatingly consented, and the results were miraculous! Within two years' time Maria's head shrank to almost normal. Soon she was able to move about in a tiny wheelchair. She could even swing.

Now seven years old, Maria holds an important and special place in the nursery. Since Maria came, the day-nursery has changed into a home for defective children. As with Maria, the Sisters accept each child as having human potential. Under their personalized love and tenderness, each child responds and develops into a personality.

Neil's parents were eager for him to do well in school. In fact, they hoped to help him through college. Neil tried very hard but could hardly pass fifth-grade work. From his progress in school and other tests available, the teacher explained that Neil would have difficulty completing his elementary school work with other children his own age. This was a real blow to Neil's parents. His sister, Sara, who was fifteen, had done very well in school, and they wanted to see Neil succeed with honors also.

Too often parents with high ambitions for worldly success rob their slow child of his self-confidence when they pressure him to get good marks at school or to go to college and into a profession. "There are many useful and dignified jobs that are best performed by people who have less than average intelligence. It's the right of every individual to grow up well enough adjusted and well enough trained to be able to handle the best job that he has the intelligence for."[49]

Daniel's parents continually compared him with his

younger brother and showed a good deal of anxiety over his slow progress in school. Discouraged and frustrated, Daniel never felt successful in anything that he did and began hating books. When his teacher arranged for him to be placed in a special fourth-grade class for slow children, he did much better. For the first time in his life he felt successful. He was able to do what was expected of him. He gained self-confidence at home because his parents made favorable comments about his progress in school instead of expressing criticism.

Success is important to children, and they feel satisfied if they can do what is expected of them, even though their achievements might be far below other children of their own age.

Children like Daniel are called "educable." They will never develop beyond fourth- or fifth-grade level, even with special training. They will benefit most from learning skills that are simple and routine.

Elsie's mother talked to a nursery teacher about Elsie's slow development. The teacher urged Elsie's mother to take her child to a children's clinic for testing. The clinic advised that Elsie might benefit from a special school for retarded children in a year or two because she would be unable to benefit from regular classes. The psychologist explained that Elsie was among the group of children called "trainable." He also said that the reason Elsie was slow in sitting, walking, talking, feeding, and toilet training was because, although she was four years old, she had a mental age like

that of many two-year-olds. In the special school Elsie
would learn to get along with other children, to improve her mastery of language, to dress herself, and to
take care of her own personal needs. The teachers
would give each child a good deal of personal attention
and help Elsie to use whatever ability she had.

"Why did this happen to Elsie? Was it my fault?" her
mother asked the psychologist. He explained that many
mothers go through stages of feeling shocked, guilty, or
resentful when they learn that their child is different.
This is needless, for the child's condition is an accident
of nature. If a mother feels guilty or responsible, she
will find it impossible to give her child the love she
needs.

There are other types of handicaps children may
have. A child may be born with cerebral palsy, deaf-
ness, or epilepsy. He may have a disfiguring birthmark,
crossed eyes, or some other deformity. If his parents
accept his handicap or deformity as of no great importance and show joy and approval of him, he will not be
overly self-conscious of his peculiarity.

In caring for your normal child you may read Dr.
Spock's books once in a while, but most of the time you
simply live happily with your children. Because you are
their mother, you *feel* the needs of your children, and
out of your mother-heart you supply these needs.

Children with handicaps will have even more than
the usual need for personal security, for being wanted,
and for being loved for their own sake. The fact that a

child's intelligence is limited may make it more important to give his emotional development special attention. Limited intelligence does not change the spiritual needs of a child.

The parent who is troubled with feelings of guilt and disappointment will see in the child a constant reminder. This conflict may disrupt the healthy balance of family living and positive feeling by the parents and children. Even parents of normal children may sometimes find it hard to accept and love their children in difficult times. It is even more likely that parents with handicapped children will sometimes have attitudes of conflict and rejection, especially when care of the child requires sacrifice and major family adjustments.

It is difficult for those of us who are friends and relatives of a family with a handicapped child to understand sympathetically the extent of the problems these handicaps may create. We can't understand why God allows these things to happen. Yet many people have found that the experience of care and sacrifice has created satisfaction and strengthening of character. New meanings have been found in life that come only from a deep giving of one's self in difficult circumstances.

A very real problem that parents of handicapped children need to face is whether they should care for their child at home or place him in a school or an institution. Parents should take their time in coming to this decision, and if they are in doubt, they can seek guidance from a family social agency or a psychiatrist. Doctors frequently advise keeping the child at home so that the family can give him the loving personal care that many institutions lack.

Few parents want children with unusually high intelligence. They prefer their children to grow up emotionally stable, with sound moral characters and social skills that will bring them acceptance by others, success, and happiness.

Ten-year-old Linda never seemed to have enough to keep her busy in fifth grade. In fact, she often disturbed other children in her class. Her teacher said she did not have enough work. Regular fifth-grade work was not well suited to Linda. The teacher gave her additional assignments that challenged her high ability.

Occasionally very bright children develop emotional problems because adjustments to the general environment may be more difficult for them than for the average child. Schools are giving more and more attention to brighter children by giving special consideration to their assignments and emotional needs. Instead of special promotion, the trend is to retain the child in the grade where he is but challenge him with extra studies, responsibilities, and activities.

Parents can challenge the gifted child through good reading material, visits to museums and industrial plants, and so on, as well as by encouraging him to learn all about his own community. Parents need to encourage him to have playmates and friends, to take his share of family projects and chores. He should take up a hobby that involves physical exercise. A balanced life of exercise, work, and play, as well as friendships, enrich his life and help to keep him from becoming a social misfit.

He should be encouraged to develop his special talents. Often it's hard for him to make up his mind because he is capable in a number of areas. His parents should not exploit him or brag about his exceptional abilities. They must accept him as a normal child and not treat him as a little adult.

An underlying basic need for the gifted child is a relaxed home relationship conducive to discussion and counsel. This helps the child to sort out his ideas, think things through, and consider the consequences.

The gifted child plus Christ—what a combination this could be!

16

The Single Parent

Carrie, a widow with four children, admits: "I'm guilty of not listening to my children. Not because I'm so involved in my own selfish thoughts, but because there are so many things to think about regarding house and children."

Susan weeps, "I have two boys, ages six and eight, who have become real discipline problems."

Reta simply states without any emotion. "I never go anywhere. I just stay at home and take care of my three preschool age children."

Jean discovered that in her loneliness she had become full of self-pity, blaming God for her unhappy situation. In such a state she was unable to be a good mother. Then one day she thought, "How can I be angry with God? He has been good to me and the children." She decided to take a positive outlook on life. She learned to accept death as a reality, realizing that life must go on for her and the children. She resolved to show her gratitude for her blessings by providing a cozy, happy home for her children. New relationships developed between Jean and her children as she discovered courage, strength, and joy in her faith. The children caught the contented, happy atmosphere she created in the home. "The joy of the Lord" is now Jean's strength.

Faith helps the single parent to face daily life, for God ". . . is a father to the fatherless; he gives justice to the widows . . . " (Psalms 68:5 LB). He is a friend who sticks closer than any person. Prayer is power. Through this avenue, the single parent can relay her problems and concerns to God who listens to both joys and sorrows. He is the source of wisdom. All she needs to do is ask Him for it.

The divorced or unwed mother must also work through her feelings about the father of her children. Only then will she have the stamina to help her children deal with their hurts and hostilities. The child from a broken home should have the opportunity to express his feelings and talk them over openly and honestly. Perhaps he feels abandoned and needs to work through his anger. Often he feels responsible for the situation. He needs the assurance that he's loved and is not to blame.

One mother discovered her small son was identifying with his older brother as a father and was afraid of the real father who came for occasional visits. Wisely, she began affirming her little boy's father. She even placed the father's picture by the child's bed. In a short time the child was eager for his father's visits.

Children who have lost a father through death need

to have direct and truthful answers to their questions. The mother needs to be understanding and sympathetic to their grief. She must be alert to fears that might grow out of the experience. The mother should be sensitive to the child's viewpoints in the decisions she makes.

It is best for the family deprived of the father to continue to relate to familiar friends and places. Authorities advise such families not to make a major move, or to sell the car and household furnishings, or to drop family friends who have always meant much to them. Keeping the dear and familiar in their daily lives helps to maintain balance and meaning in the fatherless family.

Some single parents decide to remarry immediately, and others vow never to. Neither approach is correct. Remarriage is not necessarily an escape from loneliness or from the pressures of parenting alone or from economic hardship. Help and advice from friends and assurance from God are needed before taking such a step. The single parent should wait patiently for the right time when she knows her motives and has met the right person.

It is wise to join a small group composed of people with common interests and goals. Feelings and problems can be shared in a setting such as this, and the group's understanding and concern help to resolve unhappy emotions. Through sharing, the mother receives helpful insights into her child's behavior and needs at various stages of growth. Single parents can find excellent support by joining organizations such as Parents Without Partners, Inc., an international, nonprofit, nonsectarian, educational organization devoted to the interests and welfare of single parents and their children.

The single parent who has always been a part of a church group will often find supportive persons, families, and groups within the church fellowship.

It is important to be a part of mixed groups. The single mother, whether by choice or by circumstance, needs the masculine viewpoint for balanced living—both for herself and for her children. It is important to have contact with men in informal conversational settings. Married couples should be sensitive to these needs. Too often the single mother is invited over when the husband is away, or the husband buries himself behind the newspaper or leaves the room so that the women can talk. There are many areas in which married couples can include the single mother in their social lives.

The single parent cannot be both mother and father. Doris says that when she quit trying to be both and concentrated on being a good mother, life moved more smoothly. But then she had the problem of finding a male adult who was interested in the children, and who could relate in a variety of experiences. Doris's brother helped to fill this need for her children.

A widow recalled an incident when she attended a picnic with her little girls. The fathers and children were enjoying games and playing happily together. She stood there with two of her little daughters who watched with eager eyes, but not one father asked if they would like to join them. Later, on the way to town for groceries, her seven-year-old wistfully wondered what it would be like to have a father.

Another single mother says that the grandparents of other children made life richer for her own because they "stretched their arms wider than usual." When this mother could not help her seven-year-old son to build his dream spaceship out of the tin cans he had salvaged, an older family friend took the lad to his workshop and helped him with his project. On other occasions, a neighbor couple was a source of security for her children when she had to be away from home. Through the social work program of a local college, a series of "big brothers" provided masculine activities for her son. This mother says, "Can such love be measured or even thanked?"[50]

A widow once remarked, "I have to really discipline myself, or I can get bitter and sarcastic." It's true; people won't befriend someone who is bitter or a chronic complainer. Develop a pleasing, attractive manner. The Bible says, "The one who has friends must be friendly." You'll begin to forget yourself as you become interested in serving others.

Dr. Kenneth D. Barringer, in his regular feature for single parents in the magazine *The Christian Home,* encourages them to use loneliness as an "opportunity for personal growth and development. See it as a challenge to conquer," he advises, "not as a blight over you. . . . Live fully in the here and now, not in the past or uncertain future. Enjoy today and see your struggles as the means that will make you stronger. Others have conquered loneliness. You can too."[51]

Whether one is a single parent or not, there is a stark reality we all need to remember. True happiness and contentment do not result from situations or circumstances, or from marriage or singleness, but from right relationships with God, your Maker and Friend.

17

The Chosen Child

"And whose little girl are you?" a welfare official asked a little girl in Chicago.

"I'm nobody's nothin'," she replied.

Perhaps you are a mother who is doing something for a "nobody's nothin' " who has been made homeless as a result of divorce, illegitimacy, parental abuse, neglect, or mental illness.

Sixty years ago neglected and orphaned children were hauled off to orphanages. When these orphanages were filled, the remainder of such children roamed the cities or were taken to some agricultural communities to help in kitchens and fields.

In 1909 President Theodore Roosevelt called the first White House Conference on The Care of Dependent Children. The conferees agreed that a child was better off in a family, even if it wasn't his own, than to exist in the cold, impersonal atmosphere of an institution. However, the idea of foster care did not gain universal acceptance until the mid-thirties.

Agencies look for mature couples who are not necessarily well off financially but who have a good marriage

and who love and understand children. They check the
prospective foster home for an atmosphere of warmth
and emotional stability. They try to choose families
with average faults and virtues and a bit of extra courage thrown in.

Joe and Nola Treacy are a dedicated couple who
have exhibited the genuine love and concern so necessary for foster parents to possess. In some twenty years
they have cared for more than three hundred children
of just about every nationality, color, and faith. Mr.
Treacy is a fireman in Yonkers, New York.

Frequently the foster child comes bearing the scars
of rejection. The foster parents need to accept the brunt
of the child's hurts and hostility. They need to keep a
level head and a sense of humor while they love the
child realistically and sometimes firmly.

One foster parent said, after their experience with a
teenage girl who ran away several times:

> There is a great price extracted from foster parents
> when, as Christians, we try to show the love of Christ
> to those who need it most. We must show the steady,
> *accepting* love which will finally enable her to accept the
> love of God. Only in Him can she find security.[52]

Two-year-old Paul come into a foster home with a
year-old sister. He rejected all advances of love. He was
afraid and hostile. The first week he flushed two dozen
diapers down the toilet. Had his foster parents been

overly concerned about those diapers, they would have lost Paul. As it was, they praised him for his good qualities and ignored his bad ones. After a week Paul broke the rejection barrier, and love won out.

The adjustment is not only between the foster child and his temporary parents; it will involve the other children in the home as well. Often the parents hesitate to subject their own children to all kinds of unknown dangers such as bad language, disease, and knowledge of the seamy side of life. However, one foster father said that it is a part of education for children in Christian homes to realize there is another side to life. It's a splendid teaching opportunity to show the difference it makes in homes when parents love and obey Jesus Christ. It is also an effective way to demonstrate to one's children that Christ expects us to share our love and His love with others.

After helping the child to gain security, it takes a mature and unselfish love to be prepared to part with the child when he leaves for a permanent home. One mother demonstrated this true love when, after caring for twins for thirteen months, she could say: "They had come in diapers and with clouded minds. They walk out like prince and princess. Our losing them was my great sorrow, but their return to their parents was my victory."[53]

Many times it is the father who has the most difficult task of accepting someone else's child into the home. Luke Yoder wished that his wife Marilyn's mothering could be fulfilled through their own two sons, aged ten and eight. But after months of Marilyn's persistent reasoning and knowing that taking foster children was a worthy project, he decided to give it a try. The welfare agency brought them three ragged, undernourished brothers—ages one, two, and three. This was more than Marilyn had bargained for, and when Luke saw how tired, cross, and frustrated she became in the daily care of three active children, he had to bite back the "I told you so's." Instead, he pitched in to help with tasks that he had not seen as part of his role before.

As the boys began to lose their fears and insecurities, Luke came to terms with the foster father experience. When the boys' natural parents signed surrender papers, Luke was ready to open his heart to them permanently. Luke says that not only did the three brothers find a foster father when he allowed himself to be open to the experience, but through it all he also found part of himself.[54]

As in the case of Marilyn and Luke, foster parents may find themselves adopting the child or children they have loved and cared for.

A mother of three adopted children remarked that adoption is a wonderful privilege. It is not a matter of taking care of someone else's child and therefore performing an act of charity. But rather, it is finding the child who belongs in your home, loving the child, and being loved in return. It's taking on all the responsibilities and privileges of normal parenthood. She never felt like she was caring for "someone else's" children. They are *her own!*

One day a caseworker for an adoption agency visited a home where she had placed two small children for adoption. Shortly after she had begun to chat, the small boy became sick and vomited on the floor. Prior to this, he had showed no signs of being sick or of feeling other than his usual sunny self. While the anxious mother was cleaning up the floor and trying to care for the little boy, the baby began to cry. Knowing it was time for the baby's morning nap, the mother decided to put her to bed so that she could give full attention to the boy and the caseworker. But the baby had other ideas and set off a howl of disapproval. At the same time there was a knock at the door. A friend had come to see these newly adopted children! The caseworker waited patiently during all this confusion for a chance to talk with the mother about how things were going. This young mother was thankful for a kind and understanding caseworker who was not looking for perfection in the home but who realized that normal homelife includes episodes such as these.

The caseworker is a friend of all three parties involved in an adoption case—the natural parents, the child, and the adoptive parents. The agency isn't necessarily attempting to supply a baby or child for the childless couple but is trying to find a good home for each needy child. An agency looks for a mature couple whose motive for adoption is to give their love and themselves to the child, a couple who are able to see the child as a unique human being with his or her own personality.

With the increasing shortage of adoptable babies, more and more families are taking children with physical defects or racial differences into their homes.

Many mature couples are asked to accept older children, because the adjustments are greater in this case. An adoptive parent says that it was a most rewarding experience to have an older adopted child, who was making all the adjustments, to suddenly sing out confidently as they turned into the driveway, "We're home!" or to hear her say proudly, "This is MY daddy!" Then he knew that the biggest part of her adjustment had been made and that we were well on the road to a happy life together!

Anna Bowman, who is a supervisor for Community Services in Toronto, Ontario, gives some helpful advice. When there are natural-born and adopted or foster children in the same family, she warns against the trap of explaining, "We had to take them because they were born to us, but we chose you." Statements like this can set up rivalry between the children and make the adopted one "suffer his rejection more keenly."

Miss Bowman warns against saying, "We love you all the same." Parents can love their children differently and equally but not the same. She feels that parents should help "interested minority children find out all they can about their racial backgrounds."[55]

Just as with natural parents, it helps for foster or adoptive parents to find someone they can trust to whom they can admit their fears and from whom they can ask help.

One mother who has worked with six different agencies in four states and has had twenty-six foster children in her home, suggests:

Only Christ can offer stability. Only Christ can teach them love. Only Christ can halt the downward skid. Christianity means nothing, however, to a child who does not see this answer in action and feel it in warm, accepting love. This must be embodied in a person. Perhaps this person should be you. [56]

18

The Whole Child

A child needs both father and mother. Together they share in raising the children. Each should be sensitive to the other's ideas as they together plan goals for the child.

The Creator intended the mother, by her very biological make-up, to be with the child more in the early formative years than is the father. And her influence is felt for many generations. This calls for much wisdom, much understanding, and much love. She needs to be aware of the child's total needs and how to meet them.

The sensitive, conscientious mother is sometimes tempted to compartmentalize her child. She might read the latest books on child rearing and painstakingly try to follow its guidelines in ministering to her child's physical, mental, and emotional needs. In her anxious concern to do the right thing she may overlook or overdo one of these important areas. What the child needs most in those early years is kind, tender love.

I'd like to share my own experience here. Our second son started sucking his thumb at ten months of age, after a painful mouth disease. I was horrified! In those days the books said thumb-sucking was not to be tolerated. I sewed up a flannel glove, forcing him to suck fuzzy flannel. In a short time he had sucked a hole in the glove and had his thumb in his mouth. This time I made a "snuggle bunny." Soon his thumb found its freedom through a ripped seam. I then resorted to medicine so bitter that it nearly shriveled up my own tongue. He took a suck, frowned, gave his thumb the once-over look, stuck it back into his mouth and sucked to his heart's content. I couldn't let such a terrible habit continue, so thinking it was "mother love" I started to slap his hands. He didn't stop the habit until he was nearly four years old.

My next two babies started sucking thumbs when they were only a few months old. Somewhere along the way I had had a change of mind. So completely ignoring it, I began to love and cuddle them more. I don't remember when they stopped sucking their thumbs, but it never became a fixed habit. I discovered that many of the undesirable habits and nervous traits in my children could be controlled by demonstrating more affection and love. What a child needs *most* in those early years is TLC—tender, loving care. And throughout his growth and development the mother still must be alert to all his varied needs at the different ages and stages.

In recounting his boyhood experiences, the late President Dwight D. Eisenhower related that his mother showed him step by step how to make Mexican hot tamales. Then he set up a small business making and selling hot tamales for five cents each. He didn't make a lot of money, but that didn't matter. He and his brothers could eat the ones they didn't sell. His mother had really listened to his request. She had heard her son's need for finding himself, for launching out in an independent venture. Sometimes it is difficult for a mother to stand back and allow her child to experience victories or failures of his own. Our children must learn to struggle. Jenkin Lloyd Jones wrote, "These are not good years for bawlers, whiners, and hiders-in-the-closet."[57]

A mother not only needs to listen to the child's inner cries but must identify with feelings. Children rate such a parent high—"They understand."

Miss Travers (Mary Poppins) relates this incident from when she was a young girl. While tidying up her room, her mother picked up Mary's doll from the floor and tossed it to her saying, "Put it away yourself." Mary didn't catch it and the doll broke.

Mary cried, "Mother, you've killed her!"

Weeping, her mother picked up the broken china pieces, placed her arms around her daughter and begged, "Forgive me, forgive me. I didn't mean to." She proceeded to heal her daughter's heart by showing sympathy and asking forgiveness.

Another important goal and task for a mother is to love her child's father. Parental love helps to bring security and happiness to a child. Also important is the parent's love for each other. Dr. Charlie W. Shedd, in his book *Promises to Peter,* indicates that when a father and mother love each other, the child isn't preoccupied with worry and fear. To him life is good. He expects the future will be good also.

When parents quarrel between themselves, the child usually feels guilty. He begins to think that he's the cause of their conflicts. An atmosphere of bitterness, hostility, and hate in the home results in confusion for the child. It often results in twisted personalities, severe emotional and mental problems, and, at times, sex perversion. Negative attitudes spill over into the home just as love does.

Fortunate the child whose father and mother truly love each other. Father-mother love is a major part of parental love. Love is the basis for peace, joy, patience, communication, kindness, caring, sharing, listening, and forgiveness.

It is comforting to know that regardless of how much we love our children, God loves them more. For all of the mistakes we make, God makes none. We may misunderstand, but God never does. There are no perfect parents, no perfect mothers. We needn't feel guilty because of our imperfections or our children's mistakes. Forgiveness is a part of love. As we forgive our children for their misbehavior, they will learn how to forgive us.

Forgiveness is a very important lesson in learning how to love others. We need God's help because He is the source of forgiveness, mercy, and an unselfish concern for others.

With faith and trust we hand our blunders and defeats to God, and He will turn them into blessings and victories. Now we are limited in our knowledge. We can never fully comprehend God or our child, but with God's help we can learn from mistakes. We go forward with our eyes and minds fixed on Him and His love.

The Bible pays tribute to a sincere Christian mother: "She watches carefully all that goes on throughout her household, and is never lazy. Her children stand and bless her; so does her husband. He praises her with these words: 'There are many fine women in the world, but you are the best of them all!'" (Proverbs 31:27-29 LB).

A MOTHER'S PRAYER

I do not ask riches for my children,
    Nor even recognition for their skill;
I only ask that Thou wilt give them
    A heart completely yielded to Thy will.

I do not ask for wisdom for my children
    Beyond discernment of Thy grace;
I only ask that Thou wilt use them
    In Thine own appointed place.

I do not ask for favor for my children
    To seat them on Thy left hand or Thy right;
But may they join the throng in heaven
    That sing before Thy throne so bright.

I do not seek perfection in my children,
    For then my own faults I would hide;
I only ask that we might walk together
    And serve our Saviour side by side. [58]

PHYLLIS DIDRIKSEN

Source Notes

Chapter 3

[1] *Redbook*, April, 1975, p. 99.
[2] *Redbook's Young Mother*, The McCall Publishing Company.

Chapter 4

[3] Phyllis Martens, "Stewardships of Children," ed. Helen Alderfer, *A Farthing in Her Hand* (Scottdale: Herald Press, 1964), p. 49.

Chapter 5

[4] *The Child Under Six*, James L. Hymes, Jr. (Englewood Cliffs, N.J.: Prentice-Hall, 1961), p. 172–174.

Chapter 6

[5] Bruno Bettelheim, *Quote*, February 11, 1973, p. 125.
[6] Benjamin Spock, M.D., *Ladies' Home Journal*.
[7] "Don't Throw That Box Away" by Florence Ran-

dall. Reprinted by permission from the *PTA Magazine,* June, 1959.

[8] Elizabeth Starr Hill, *Evan's Corner* (New York: Holt, Rinehart and Winston, 1967), p. 28.

[9] Alta Mae Erb, "Creativity: God's Gift to Children," *Christian Living,* August, 1969. Used by permission.

[10] *Ibid.*

[11] Jean Todd Freeman, "Games Children Don't Play" *Ladies' Home Journal,* March, 1969, p. 166.

[12] Erb, *op. cit.*

[13] Georgie Starbuck Galbraith, Reprinted from *Ladies' Home Journal.*

Chapter 7

[14] Phyllis Martens, "Stewardships of Children," ed. Helen Alderfer, *A Farthing in Her Hand* (Scottdale: Herald Press, 1964), p. 51, 52.

[15] Benjamin Spock, *Baby and Child Care* (New York: Simon and Schuster, 1968), p. 330.

[16] Phyllis McGinley, "The Casual Touch," *Sixpence in Her Shoe* (New York: Dell Publishing Co., 1966), p. 229.

[17] *Ibid.,* p. 230.

[18] Mary Rempel, "Stewardship of Speech," ed. Helen Alderfer, *A Farthing in Her Hand* (Scottdale: Herald Press, 1964), p. 119.

Chapter 8

[19] Marlene Kropf, "Help Your Child to Choose His Heroes," *Christian Living,* November, 1974, p. 29.

[20] Jean Karl, *From Childhood to Childhood* (New York: The John Day Company, 1971), p. 7.

[21] *Ibid.*

[22] *Ibid.,* p. 8.

[23] *Ibid.*

[24] Annis Duff, *Longer Flight,* New York: Viking Press, Inc., 1955.

[25] Maud and Miska Petersham, *The Christ Child,* New York: Doubleday Co., Inc. 1931.

Chapter 9

[26] John Drescher, "Children Need a Sense of Significance," *Mennonite Brethren Herald,* August 22, 1975, p. 26.

[27] *Ibid.*

[28] "For Your Children a Gift of Time," Helen Lescheid, *Christian Living,* December, 1972, p. 8.

[29] *Ibid.*

[30] "Self-Esteem for the Child," *Family Life,* ed. Paul Popenoe, Vol. 34, No. 4, July-August, 1974.

[31] "Mom, Dad, Am I Doing Okay?" Ray and Clara Keim, *Christian Living,* February, 1974, p. 17.

[32] "Self-Esteem for the Child," *Family Life,* Vol. 34, No. 4, July-August, 1974.

[33] Haim G. Ginott, *Between Parent and Child* (New York: Avon, 1969), p. 20.

Chapter 10

[34] Marlene Kropf, "Help Your Child to Choose His Heroes," *Christian Living,* November, 1974, p. 30.

[35] Elizabeth Yoder, "One Way to Share Faith With Children," *Christian Living,* February, 1976, p. 24.

[36] *Ibid.,* p. 26.

[37] *Ibid.,* p. 26.

[38] *Ibid.,* p. 26.

Chapter 11

[39] Benjamin Spock, *Baby and Child Care* (New York: Simon and Schuster, 1968), p. 302.

[40] Jean Eash, "How I Am Getting My Family off Snack Foods," *Christian Living,* February, 1974, p. 20.

[41] Beatitudes for Homemakers." A *Heart to Heart* publication.

Chapter 12

[42] Sara Wengerd, "How to Childproof Your Home," *Christian Living, September, 1973, p. 7.*

[43] Benjamin Spock, *Baby and Child Care* (New York: Simon and Schuster, 1968), p. 537.

[44] *Ibid.,* p. 268.

[45] *Ibid.,* p. 541.

Chapter 13

[46] Charles Waugaman, *Christian Living*, February, 1975, p. 29. Used by permission.

Chapter 14

[47] Mildred Tengbom, "How to Help the Bereaved Child," *Christian Living*, February, 1975, p. 22.
[48] Janette Klopfenstein, "How to Help in Time of Death," *Christian Living*, July, 1974, p. 17.

Chapter 15

[49] Benjamin Spock, *Baby and Child Care* (New York: Simon and Schuster, 1968), p. 581.

Chapter 16

[50] Katie Funk Wiebe, "Who Will Help Me Raise My Children?" *Christian Living*, December, 1974, p. 32.
[51] *The Christian Home*, November, 1973, p. 48.

Chapter 17

[52] *The Christian Reader*, April-May, 1967, p. 6.
[53] *Time*, October 27, 1961, p. 60.
[54] Janette Klopfenstein, "A Foster Father Finds Himself," *Christian Living*, December, 1974, p. 6-10.
[55] Sue Steiner, "What It Takes to Be an Adoptive Parent," *Christian Living*, January, 1974, p. 23-25.
[56] *The Christian Reader*, April-May, 1967, p. 8.

Chapter 18

[57] Jenkin Lloyd Jones, "Teach Your Child to 'Love the Storm' " *Reader's Digest,* February, 1963, p. 127.

[58] Phyllis Didriksen, From *Sourcebook for Mothers,* compiled by Eleanor Doan (Grand Rapids, Mich.: Zondervan Publishing House, 1969), p. 66.